A+ Certification
Success Guide

A+ Certification Success Guide

For Computer Technicians

Sarah T. Parks
Bob Kalman

McGraw-Hill

New York San Francisco Washington, D.C. Auckland Bogotá
Caracas Lisbon London Madrid Mexico City Milan
Montreal New Delhi San Juan Singapore
Sydney Tokyo Toronto

McGraw-Hill

A Division of The McGraw-Hill Companies

pbk   1 2 3 4 5 6 7 8 9 FGR/FGR 9 0 0 9 8 7 6

hc   1 2 3 4 5 6 7 8 9 FGR/FGR 9 0 0 9 8 7 6

ISBN 0-07-048596-8 (pbk)
ISBN 0-07-048595-X (hard)

McGraw-Hill books are available at special quantity discounts to use as premiums and sales promotions, or for use in corporate training programs. For more information, please write to the Director of Special Sales, McGraw-Hill, 11 West 19th Street, New York, NY 10011. Or contact your local bookstore.

Technical editor: Lawrence Gilius
Reviewers: Elizabeth G. Berglund, Director of Marketing Communications, CompTIA;
          and Rick Brown, Manager of Technical Support for Conner Peripherals and
          Chairman of the A+ Development Committee
Acquisitions editor: Brad Schepp
Editorial team: David Learn, Book Editor
          David M. McCandless, Associate Managing Editor
          Lori Flaherty, Executive Editor
          Joann Woy, Indexer
Production team: Katherine G. Brown, Director
          Susan E. Hansford, Coding
          Brenda M. Plasterer, Coding
          Rhonda E. Baker, Desktop Operator
          Nancy K. Mickley, Proofreading
          Jeffrey Hall, Computer Artist
          Brenda S. Wilhide, Computer Artist
Design team: Jaclyn J. Boone, Designer
          Katherine Lukaszewicz, Associate Designer

0485968
WK2

To Craig and Todd with love, and thanks to Bob for his patience.
Sarah T. Parks

To my heavenly Father for the blessings he has bestowed upon me; to Frank and Marian Kalman, who provided a foundation and guidance in my life; to my children Bethany and Bob for the joy and gladness they have brought into my life; and to Barbara for all her love and support. I love you all.
Bob Kalman

Contents

Appendices

Acknowledgments

The authors gratefully acknowledge the contributions of the following people:

AST

Michael Beach, Data Source / Connecting Point

William S. Beasley, Zenith Data Systems

Barbara Beelen, Kraft Foods

Elizabeth G. Berglund, Director of Marketing Communications, CompTIA

Rick Brown, Manager of Technical Support for Conner Peripherals and Chairman of the A+ Development Committee

Stephen Clancy, Dataquest

Kenneth W. Conn, Data Source / Connecting Point

Lex Darr, Vanstar Corporation

Galen Davis, Intel Corporation

Greg Dodge, Dataflex

Mariano Dy-Liacco, Dataflex

Bob Evans, Self Test Software

Acknowledgments

Jim Frey, Zenith Data Systems

John Hlavac, Packard Bell

Alan Hupp, Sylvan Prometric

Marilyn Martin, Sylvan Prometric

Sharon Martin, Apple Computer, Inc.

David S. McWilliams, Packard Bell

Micrografx, Inc.

Craig Parks

Mary Pizzo, Apple Computer, Inc.

Mark D. Romanowski, US Computer Group, Inc.

Todd Schwartz

Bill Strathearn, OURS

John Venator, Executive Vice President and CEO, CompTIA

Aaron Woods

Bill York, CompUSA

Introduction

CompUSA, a major microcomputer reseller, now requires all of its service employees to be A+ certified within 90 days of employment. Packard Bell, a manufacturer, demands the same of its new service employees. Wang Laboratories, a major provider of computer services, requires A+ of all its engineers with PC-support responsibilities, and Microsoft Corporation hires no computer technicians who are not A+ certified.

Support for the A+ program comes from all corners of the industry and is growing steadily. Original supporters in 1993 included, among others, Apple, Compaq, Hewlett-Packard, Toshiba, and Digital Equipment Corporation, along with the industry's major service organization: the Association for Field Service Management International. That group has been joined by many others. Newest supporters include AST Research, Aerotek-Data Service Group, and Lotus Development.

The ranks of the A+ certified grow rapidly. In the last half of 1993, computer service professionals took 1,949 A+ exams. In the first half of 1994, they took 4,601 A+ exams, and that number was slightly surpassed in the second half of 1994. In just the first four months of

1995, they took an additional 5,197 A+ exams. As of November, 1995, 16,601 computer service technicians were A+ certified.

Why so much interest in the A+ program? The credential is the first available to computer service technicians that allows them to prove they have the basic skills needed to succeed in their profession. It documents competence on a range of fundamental service skills such as configuring, installing and upgrading, diagnosing, repairing, and maintaining computer equipment and peripherals. Further, the fundamental skills certified by A+ are valid and useful regardless of the brand name on the machinery—they apply equally well to the products of any vendor.

As such, the A+ certification plays an important role in the information technology (IT) industry, benefiting everyone interested in offering or using the skills of a professional computer service technician. For example, vendors use A+ to ensure high quality among those who sell and service their products. Resellers enjoy the way A+ allows their technicians to "test out" of basic training requirements imposed by vendors whose products they represent. This dramatically reduces training time and cost. And customers prefer working with resellers who can support their claims of professionalism with A+ certification.

As a result, computer service technicians find that they are more valuable to their employers after becoming A+ certified, whether their employer is a vendor, reseller, or end-user organization. For many technicians, new avenues to employment, promotions, and improved earnings open once they've earned the credential.

This book is an important resource for you, the computer service professional aiming for A+ certification. It will help you to understand the process of becoming A+ certified, learn important technical knowledge that could be helpful in passing the A+ exams, and then use your new credential to greatest benefit in your career.

Chapter 1 gives you all the information you need to get started. It explains the A+ certification program—what it is, why it was created, and the organization that sponsors it. Then it gives you the detailed, action-oriented information you need to get going: how to register, how to prepare, and hints on how to take your A+ exams.

Chapter 2 steps back to give you the bigger picture. It explains the trend toward certification, and toward A+ certification in particular, by examining the benefits of the A+ certification to every player in the IT industry. Once you know who benefits and why, you'll be in a better position to use your new certification with greater leverage in your career.

Chapter 3 examines the rapidly changing marketplace for IT skills, identifies the major employers of computer service technicians, and shows how A+ certification helps address the need for top-quality service.

Chapter 4 helps prepare you to take the A+ core exam. Its study materials are organized by the major technologies tested on the exam, including microcomputers, displays, storage media, printers, basic operating systems (DOS, Windows, Macintosh), modems, buses, and CD-ROMs. Also, each of the six major duty areas of the technician that are covered on the core exam are also covered in Chapter 4 as they relate to each of these technologies. Chapter 4 concludes with sample exam questions that give you valuable exam practice and important feedback on your skill level.

Chapter 5 helps prepare you to take the Microsoft Windows/DOS specialty exam (candidates for A+ certification currently need to pass the core exam, which tests skills that are not vendor-specific, and one of two specialty exams). This chapter is organized by the four major categories of skill tested on this specialty exam. Subsections of the material correspond with each of the individual skills or abilities that the examiners have determined to be needed for success in working with Microsoft Windows or DOS technologies. The chapter concludes with sample test questions for this specialty exam.

Chapter 6 helps prepare you to take the Macintosh OS-based computers specialty exam. Like Chapter 5, it is organized both by the major skill categories tested on the exam and by the individual skills identified by the examiners as crucial to success with these particular technologies. This chapter also concludes with a set of sample exam questions.

This book's appendices have been designed to be particularly useful as a supplement to the book. Appendix A lists the A+ Cornerstone

Funding Partners and Sponsors. Appendix B gives information on how a service center as a whole can earn the special designation of A+ Authorized Service Center.

Because this book cannot possibly contain all the technical information one could conceivably need to review in order to prepare to pass each of the three A+ exams, Appendix C provides a valuable list of supplementary books (and some films) recommended by dozens of vendors, resellers, and IT trainers who are intimately familiar with the A+ exam. It also lists books that will be helpful to your career, covering such topics as resumes, cover letters, and interviewing. Appendix D lists sources of classroom and computer-based training opportunities for those who may need them.

Appendix E summarizes the guidelines for using the A+ certification name and logo to identify yourself once you've earned your certification. Appendix F presents the job profile of a service technician developed by the sponsors of the A+ exam. This important document identifies the major skills needed for success in every area of activity undertaken by service technicians today. Some of the skills identified in this profile are not easily tested and therefore do not appear on the A+ exams. The appendix presents the job profile and discusses the areas not tested on the current version of the A+ exam, including business management, administration, and professionalism. Finally, Appendix G presents the latest research results about the value of certification.

No other single resource offers so much information about the A+ program and its exams. For many, this resource will be the only one they need in order to pass the A+ exams and begin to enjoy the many benefits that go with A+ certification. Others who need to go beyond this book for further reading and instruction will find in this book significant help in identifying their current strengths and weaknesses and directing them on toward the most useful supplementary resources. Either way, this book will help you to earn and use your A+ certification. And earning that certification may be one of the most important things you can do for your career.

We wish you every success.

Becoming
A+ certified

CHAPTER 1

THIS chapter gives you an overview of everything you need to know and do to become A+ certified. It explains what A+ certification is, who it's for, and the purposes it serves. It also gives you the information you need in order to register and pay for your exam, use the study materials in this book, and select other resources that can help you get ready. Finally, it prepares you to study effectively for the exam, take it, and know what to expect afterwards.

What is A+ certification?

A+ certification is a way for microcomputer service technicians to prove their competence by earning a nationally recognized credential. A+ certification is awarded based upon successful completion of the A+ certification exams sponsored by the Computing Technology Industry Association. The program is backed by major vendors, distributors, resellers, and publications, as well as a leading industry service organization, the Association of Field Service Management, Inc.

The exams test the basic knowledge, technical skills, and customer interaction skills needed by a successful computer service technician, as defined by over 45 organizations in the information technology industry. The exams cover a broad range of hardware and software technologies, but do not test knowledge of vendor-specific products.

There are no specific requirements for A+ candidates before they sit for the exams, which are geared to those with at least six months' experience. However, many candidates have several years' experience, while others may need training programs in order to pass the A+ exams.

To become A+ certified, candidates must pass two tests: the Core exam and one of two other Specialty exams, either the Microsoft Windows/DOS Specialty Exam or the Macintosh OS-based Computers Specialty Exam. When candidates pass the Core exam plus a Specialty exam, they receive a certificate that mentions the Specialty exam they passed, such as:

➢ A+ certification Exam with a specialty in Microsoft Windows/DOS environments

➤ A+ certification Exam with a specialty in Macintosh OS-based Computers

Those who were already A+ certified when the Specialty exams were introduced in April, 1995 need not retake the tests to remain A+ certified.

 # Who sponsors the exam?

The sponsor of the exam—the Computing Technology Industry Association (CompTIA), based in Lombard, Illinois—is a not-for-profit international trade association with over 6,000 members. CompTIA can be reached at

450 East 22nd Street, Suite 230
Lombard, Illinois 60148
(708) 268-1818

Members of the Association, located in all 50 states and Canada, represent every major company that manufactures, distributes, publishes, or resells computer-related products and services. CompTIA's role as an industry-wide umbrella organization is to promote professional competence, sound business practices, and fair and honest treatment of customers, resellers, and vendors. CompTIA committees, sections, and task forces address issues affecting the entire computer industry.

One of the most important of CompTIA's several special interest groups—its service section—first developed the industry-wide standard warranty reimbursement claim form. It went on to create the A+ certification program in order to certify technicians on a set of fundamental service and support skills. The A+ certification program is the first program to set industry-wide standards without a vendor-specific product focus.

CompTIA was recently named to the "Associations Advance America" Honor Roll by the American Society of Association Executives. Among the programs that CompTIA was honored for is the A+ certification program.

 # Why the A+ certification program?

The A+ certification program began in April, 1993, in a time of declining customer confidence in the distribution channels for information technology (IT) products and services. Research indicated that customers increasingly hesitated to seek out technical support because service providers were unable to consistently meet their expectations for quality service.

The cost of losing customers is also emerging through research. The cost of securing a new customer is at least five times that of keeping a current one; the cost to regain lost customers is approximately 25 times that of keeping current ones.

The entire industry bears the cost of losing customer confidence because the industry is built on customer acceptance and use of new technologies. If the industry cannot adequately service those technologies, industry growth suffers.

Customer confidence is critical to industry health, and that confidence is closely related to the skill of IT technicians, as a study conducted by CompTIA demonstrated. The survey of over 500 end users indicated that the greatest factor influencing customer satisfaction is the technical skills of the reseller.

The A+ certification program seeks to restore customer confidence by certifying the base skill level of computer technicians, and thereby helping the channel to hold on to current customers and more easily secure new ones. In effect, a respected outside agency is verifying through exam results that a vendor or reseller has the technical skills to back up its marketing promises with action. A+ exam content also goes beyond technical skills into areas of customer interaction, ethics, industry understanding, and professionalism—areas which are crucial to building customer confidence.

The A+ certification helps customers, vendors, and resellers, but it also helps technicians by building confidence in their own skills. It also gives

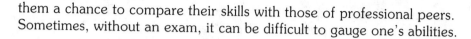

them a chance to compare their skills with those of professional peers. Sometimes, without an exam, it can be difficult to gauge one's abilities.

The A+ exams not only point out one's weaknesses, but give a sense of the range and depth of skills needed to be successful as a computer service technician. The A+ exam content areas, and the related Job Profile of a Service Technician, give an overview of needed skills. With such an overview, one can more easily assess what skills one has, and what skills one needs to develop through education, training, or experience.

The A+ exam content areas are explained in Chapters 4–6; the Job Profile of a Service Technician is presented in Appendix F.

A+ certification meets three fundamental goals of CompTIA for improving the professionalism of the IT industry to:

➤ Increase consumer confidence in the reseller channel

➤ Build individual competency for computer service technicians

➤ Develop a framework for technicians' professional growth

For further discussion about the value of A+ certification to all players in the IT industry, see Chapter 2.

⇨ How the A+ program was developed

To answer the need for an industry-wide service technician certification, CompTIA's Service & Support Section invited support from a broad base of participants. Those participants included manufacturers, distributors, resellers, third party maintenance companies, value-added resellers, industry associations, and others. Industry supporters contributed knowledge to help develop the exam, financial resources to fund the program, and commitments to promote the program in the marketplace.

Cornerstone Funding Partners—the main participants to develop and administer the program—were required to commit a minimum

investment of time, expertise, and financial resources. Other companies acted as sponsors, having a lesser commitment than the Cornerstone Funding Partners, and endorsing the program. Both Cornerstone Funding Partners and sponsors contributed their expertise to help define the baseline skills and standards to be tested by the A+ exam. A list of Cornerstone Funding Partners and current sponsors is given in Appendix A.

CompTIA asked both Cornerstone Funding Partners and sponsors for written commitments to help promote A+ certification among their employees and channel partners. In response, Digital Equipment Corporation now requires all employees who service microcomputers and related hardware to become A+ certified, as well as all computer service technicians who work for authorized service providers.

COMPAQ Computer vigorously promotes A+ certification to its own workforce. Today, the great majority of its phone support and case management personnel, along with technical trainers and selected system engineers, are A+ certified. The company also requires A+ certification of its service authorized partners.

IBM uses A+ as a prerequisite for certain hardware requirements for service providers. Apple Computer, Digital Equipment Corporation, and many others accept the A+ certification as a way for service providers to "test-out" of some or all requirements for basic training on their products. Beyond the original Cornerstone Funding Partners and sponsors, many other companies have established an A+ requirement, often in response to the demand of the marketplace.

In addition, hundreds of resellers have taken advantage of the opportunity to be designated as A+ Authorized Service Centers by having 50% or more of their staff earn the credential. (For more information on A+ Authorized Service Centers, see Appendix B.)

To organize the contributions of the diverse Cornerstone Funding Partners and Sponsors, CompTIA divided its Service & Support Section into three groups: the A+ Advisory Team, the A+ Working Team, and the A+ Item Writing Panel.

The A+ Advisory Team, made up of senior managers from the Cornerstone Funding Partners, determines the program's overall

direction. The A+ Working Team members, representing both Cornerstone Funding Partners and Sponsors, establish the specific requirements of the certification program and examination. They do this in coordination with Sylvan Prometric, the IT industry's leading provider of exam development, delivery, and administration.

The A+ Item Writing Panel includes the technology-oriented subject matter experts who have experience as service technicians or as service trainers. This team works with Sylvan Prometric to write the test items used in the A+ certification exam.

In creating the A+ certification exam, test developers made every effort to adhere to the Standards for Educational and Psychological Tests established by the American Psychological Association, the American Educational Research Association, and the National Council on Measurement in Education. The creation of test requirements and the writing of test items follow a series of steps to ensure that the exam measures the right skills in the right way.

As a first step, a great variety of jobs held by IT service technicians were examined, and the skills actually used in those jobs were defined. Then the skills were weighted to determine how much of the exam should be devoted to each. Test questions were written to measure those skills, and sample tryouts were made of the questions. Finally the exam's pass/fail standards, or the "cut score" was established.

The development of the A+ certification exam is ongoing. New exam questions are continually being written, and old ones removed. And the exam is continually reevaluated for its effectiveness in measuring who has the desired skills and who doesn't. At the same time, the skills that the exam measures are being reviewed for appropriateness. The work of computer service technicians is constantly changing, and the A+ certification exam changes to keep pace.

The popularity of the program has exceeded expectations. The A+ certification program was originally projected to certify 5,000 technicians by the end of its first year or June 1, 1994. By July, 1994, however, there were more than 6,785 A+ certified technicians. By November, 1995, 16,601 computer service technicians had become A+ certified. This is a significant percentage of the estimated

60,000 PC hardware field-service technicians in the U.S. (That 60,000 excludes technicians working on application software, UNIX hardware and software, LANs, and hotline/help desk telephone staff.)

Alan Hupp, Vice President of Marketing for Sylvan Prometric, says that the A+ certification program is "off to one of the fastest starts of any program we have administered in the information technology industry."

 # Test content and format

The content of all three A+ exams has been selected to represent the kinds of activities typically undertaken by an IT service technician. The core exam content covers procedures and information about technologies that are not related to vendor-specific products.

The two specialty exams focus on service tasks related to operating system environments commonly encountered in the industry: Microsoft Windows/DOS environments and the Mac operating system. Even though the three tests cover fundamental knowledge and skills, they are still challenging.

The core exam is currently divided into six sections with groups of related questions. Each section corresponds with one of the major areas of job responsibility for technicians. These sections are:

> ➤ Configuring

> ➤ Installing and upgrading

> ➤ Diagnosing

> ➤ Repairing

> ➤ Performing preventive maintenance

> ➤ Maintaining safety

Note that the Customer Interaction Skills area was included in past exams and will be included again in future exams, perhaps as early as spring, 1996. For the latest information about the A+ exams, contact the official exam registrar, Sylvan Prometric, at 1-800-77-MICRO (1-800-776-4276).

The specific skills tested for each category of activity on the core exam are explained in Chapter 4. Within the six areas of responsibility, the core exam also tests knowledge of the following technologies, again without reference to vendor-specific products except in the area of basic operating systems:

➢ Microcomputers

➢ Displays

➢ Storage media

➢ Printers

➢ Basic operating systems (DOS, Windows, Macintosh)

➢ Modems

➢ Buses

➢ CD-ROM

The Microsoft Windows/DOS specialty exam and the Mac OS-based computers specialty exam are each divided into four sections representing the major job responsibilities in servicing these technologies. The four sections are:

➢ Configuring

➢ Installing and upgrading

➢ Diagnosing

➢ Repairing

The specific skills tested for each category on the Microsoft Windows/DOS specialty exam are explained in Chapter 5, and the specific skills tested for each category on the Mac OS-based computers specialty exam are explained in Chapter 6.

The exams are administered on computer at a Sylvan authorized testing center, in an easy-to-use format. (The testing centers and their use of computers are explained further in separate sections below.)

The format of the tests on the computer looks very much like other multiple-choice exams you have taken before. The difference is that

you take this exam on a desktop computer connected to a testing network, where all the data is stored centrally and securely.

Directions for using the testing software are displayed on the screen. A tutorial is provided, and a proctor also assists with questions. On-screen "help" is also available, including information at the bottom of the screen that lets you know how to enter your answer, move forward in the test, or mark a question for answering later.

The A+ Core exam includes approximately 78 questions, all multiple choice. The exact set of questions on this and the Specialty exams is different for every person who is tested. Candidates have 1 hour and 15 minutes to complete the Core exam.

The Microsoft Windows/DOS Specialty Exam includes approximately 58 questions, all multiple choice. Candidates have 60 minutes to complete this exam. The Mac OS-based computers specialty exam has approximately 50 test questions. Candidates have 45 minutes to complete this exam. (Exam length and number of questions may change over time. Contact Sylvan Prometric for the most up-to-date information about the exam structure.)

Questions on both the core exam and the specialty exams are all multiple choice; however, some questions have only one correct answer, whereas others have more than one correct answer. Each question has either a circle or a square next to it. Those questions with circles have only one correct answer; those with squares have more than one correct answer. Also, when there are multiple correct answers, a message at the bottom of the screen tells you to "choose all that apply." When questions have more than one correct answer, you must select all correct answers in order to have that question scored "correct."

There are three formats for questions on the A+ exams. These are:

> Situational

> Traditional

> Identification

Situational questions describe a situation or scenario commonly encountered by service technicians while on the job. Your choice of answers will list different ways to resolve the problem or situation.

Example: When you power up the system, the attached display remains blank. You're not sure whether it is a system unit or a display problem, but you can quickly decide which it is by:

a. Turning the contrast control all the way up to the test position.

b. Installing a wrap connector onto the end of the display cable.

c. Unplugging the signal cable from the system unit, then powering the display.

d. Running the video tests on the diagnostic diskette.

The correct answer is "c."

Traditional multiple-choice questions appear most commonly on the test. These questions ask you to pick the correct answer to a short question from a list of choices.

Example: What component determines the type of monitor to be used?

a. Parallel controller.

b. Memory board.

c. Serial controller.

d. Video controller.

The correct answer is "d."

Identification questions may include a diagram, flowchart, or illustration with several items called out with arrows, numbers or letters. You are asked to choose the answer that correctly identifies what is being shown or described in the question.

Example:

The item pointed out is a ____?

    a. Battery

    b. Central processing unit

    c. Floppy disk drive

    d. Mass storage

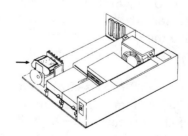

The correct answer is "a."

Practice with exam questions for each of the three A+ exams is provided at the end of Chapters 4, 5, and 6.

 # Tips for test-taking

Here are six points to remember when taking multiple-choice tests such as A+:

> Answer all questions. An unanswered question is scored as an incorrect answer.

> Guess if you have to. There is no penalty for guessing.

> Answer the easy questions first. The testing software lets you move forward and backward through the exam. Go through all the questions on the test once, answering those you are sure of first, then go back and spend time on the harder questions.

> Don't try to "psych-out" the questions. There are no trick questions. The correct answer will always be among the list of choices.

> Eliminate the most obvious incorrect answers first. This will make it easier for you to select the answer that seems most right to you.

> And finally, remember that if you don't pass this time, you can take the exam again for an additional fee.

 # Who may take the tests?

A+ certification is open to anyone who would like to take the tests. There are no requirements for taking them other than payment of the test fees. Candidates may retake the test modules as often as they like. To receive the certification, the candidate must pass the Core and one Specialty exam within 90 days of each other.

If candidates fail to pass both exams within 90 days, they will not be granted certification. Instead, they will retake the core exam—even if they had already passed it—as well as the other specialty exam. Any of the three exams may be taken as many times as needed until

certification requirements are met. (The only restriction is that the same exam cannot be retaken on the same day.) Candidates may take the core exam and both specialty exams if they choose to.

Candidates may take the core and a specialty exam in any sequence; however, it is recommended that they take the core before the specialty exam. The candidate may take the core and specialty exam or exams during the same appointment. The test developers, in fact, recommend this, although it is not required.

 # How to pay and register

The fee for taking the A+ certification tests depends on whether or not the candidate is employed by an organization that is a member of CompTIA. Additionally, taking two or three exam modules at one seating saves money. The current pricing schedule is:

	For those employed by CompTIA member organizations	For nonmembers
Any module alone	$ 90	$100
Core + 1 module	$150	$165
Core + 2 modules	$195	$215
2 modules	$150	$165

Payment for the exam can be made by Visa, Master Card, American Express, or by check. To pay, contact Sylvan Prometric at 1-800-77-MICRO to talk to a Sylvan Registrar.

Have the following information handy when you call:

➤ Social Security number (or Sylvan ID number)

➤ Complete mailing address and phone number

➤ Employer or organization

➤ Date you want to take the test

➤ Method of payment

Note: Social Security number is not required. If a candidate objects to providing a social security number for privacy reasons, Sylvan supplies a unique Sylvan ID number instead.

Often the candidate's employer will have paid for the exam in advance by purchasing vouchers from Sylvan. In that case, the candidate needs only to supply Sylvan with the voucher number to complete payment.

Once guaranteed payment is made, the test can be scheduled. Those paying with credit card or voucher can schedule immediately; those paying with check can call back to schedule three days after mailing the check. Note that cancellations are refundable if made by close of business on the day before the exam.

The Sylvan registrar helps candidates to schedule their tests at the most convenient testing center and time. Sylvan operates approximately 900 testing centers worldwide, and candidates have access to any of them they choose. Many of the testing centers are open during and after normal business hours and on weekends. Those taking their exam more than four days after they register will receive in the mail a confirmation of their test location and time.

When you first contact Sylvan registration, an electronic file of information will be built with your name, address, phone, fax number, and social security number. This eliminates the need to gather redundant data with every registration. Over time, the complete record of your testing history will be kept for you as well.

Once the registrar has you on file, you need only tell them the exam you are registering for.

 # Options for test preparation

Chapters 4, 5, and 6 of this book present useful information about all of the skills and all of the technologies tested on the three A+ exams. Of course, the range of material covered by the A+ exams is vast, and no one book can capture all of the knowledge that could be tested. For many, this book will be enough to give them the knowledge, familiarity with the test, and confidence they need to pass the A+ exams. Others

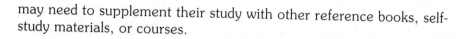

may need to supplement their study with other reference books, self-study materials, or courses.

If after using the study materials presented in this book and taking the sample test questions, you feel the need for further study, you might begin with the resources listed in Appendix C. These books and films are recommended by leading consultants, trainers, and IT organizations to those preparing for the A+ exam.

For those wanting more formal training for the A+ exams, several classroom courses are available. A variety of computer-based courses and other self-study materials are available also. A list of these resources is given in Appendix D.

How to study

The amount of study needed to pass the A+ certification exams varies greatly from one candidate to another, depending primarily on the amount of time one has spent as a practicing computer service technician.

Those with several years of experience may need only a quick review of materials in this book before passing the A+ exams on the first try. Very experienced technicians, in fact, may want to try the sample questions before even reading Chapters 4, 5, and 6, then read only the materials on the subject areas they had trouble with on the sample questions. Those new to the field may need to carefully study this entire book, then turn to supplementary resources.

Most of those preparing for the test will need to spend many hours identifying weaknesses in understanding and skill and then gaining new knowledge in those areas. For those undertaking such study, we offer the following suggestions:

Honor the way your mind works. Study when you're well rested and free from distractions, and don't try to study more than 1½ to 2 hours at a time. Too much study at any one sitting is fatiguing, frustrating, and counterproductive. Try to study at the same time each day; regular study time trains the mind to be ready to learn new material.

Make the environment right for learning. Ideally, you'll want to study in an area dedicated especially for it: a private, quiet study or home office. If you can't have that environment at home, then try using your company office after normal business hours. If that fails, try the library. In any case, study in an environment where you'll be least likely to feel pulled to do chores or respond to the needs of family members or coworkers. Choose a comfortable, efficient environment that will make your study time really focused and productive.

Set goals for each study session. Review the kinds of progress you make from one study session to the next and set ambitious, but realistic goals for each session based on your past track record. Set goals to inspire yourself, but don't strain to achieve them. Know where you would like to be in the material by the end of the session, but allow yourself the time realistically needed to absorb the information.

Use a variety of study techniques. Talking, listening, writing, reading, and working on the computer use different areas of the brain. Using each of these methods will reinforce your learning and make it stick. Some ways to employ a variety of study techniques: discuss the materials you're studying with your coworkers; have someone quiz you; recite out loud facts you're trying to memorize; use your computer as a study tool to illustrate or further investigate topics raised in the materials.

 # Taking the test

After you register, the only thing you must do is show up to take the test. Bring two forms of identification, both with signatures and one with a photo. For example, you might bring a valid driver's license or passport as a photo ID, and a major credit card as a secondary ID.

Books, calculators, laptop computers, or other reference materials are not allowed during any A+ test. Because the tests are computer-based, you will not need pens, pencils, or paper.

Arrive early at the testing center to have plenty of time to settle down and make yourself comfortable.

To allow candidates to get familiar with the various question types and how to answer them, an on-line tutorial is available to use before the test. All testing appointments include an extra 15 minutes to sign-in and use the tutorial.

The tutorial is connected to the test to be taken and teaches specifically how to answer the kinds of questions that will appear in that test. The A+ exams offer question types including multiple-choice single-answer and multiple-choice multiple-answer. On-line graphics and exhibits also sometimes appear within questions. Your tutorial explains and gives examples of these question types.

The center administrator is also available to help with the tutorial and ensure that candidates understand how to answer questions. In addition, on-line help is always available during the exam.

Sylvan delivers tests using a sophisticated yet easy-to-use Windows-based computerized testing system. Directions for using the testing software are displayed on the screen.

Figure 1-1 shows a typical format for questions.

Figure 1-1

Item 3 of 14 ▲
☐ **Mark**   **Current Time: 10:50:27 AM**

What is the official language of Ivory Coast?

○ a. Akan

◉ b. French

○ c. Kiswahili

○ d. Kikuyu

Select the best answer.

| Next | Previous | Help |

Sample test question. Sylvan Prometric

In addition to on-line help, these features have been built into the testing system for ease of use:

➢ Answers can be selected with keyboard or mouse.

➢ Candidates can mark questions for later review.

➢ The software keeps a record of questions not fully answered and prompts the candidate to review them.

➢ Candidates can review any question before the test is complete.

➢ An on-screen clock reminds of time remaining.

➢ Every answer is immediately and automatically backed up by the system in case power is lost or the system is interrupted.

The test may be completed without answering all questions; however, any unanswered question will be scored as incorrect. If you finish the exam before the time limit, you may leave. If time runs out, the exam automatically ends.

After the test

As soon as you complete the test, your exam results are shown to you on-screen. In addition, a hard copy of the score report is printed for you at the test center and embossed to indicate that it is an official score report.

The score report has two pages. The first page is the Testing Fee Reimbursement Form, which you can use if your employer is reimbursing you for your test fee. The second page is the report showing the score needed to pass your exam and your score. You will also see the percentage of questions that you answered correctly in each section, but you will not see the specific questions that you missed.

No other printed report of exam results is made; CompTIA receives results electronically from Sylvan. No one else will see the report except the testing center Administrator.

The score report will look like what's in Figs. 1-2 and 1-3.

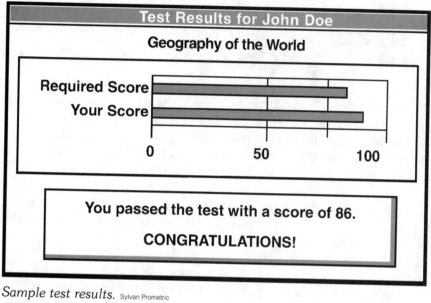

Figure 1-2

Sample test results. Sylvan Prometric

Section Scores for JOHN DOE
Geography of the World

Section Title	0	100	Score
Flags of the World			100
Geography of Europe			100
Geography of the Americas			50
Continental Geography			100
Animals of the World			0
Capitals of the World			50
Languages of the World			100
Rivers and Lakes of the World			50

OK   Help

Figure 1-3

Sample test results by sections. Sylvan Prometric

After you pass the Core exam and one Specialty exam, an A+ certificate will be mailed to you within the next two to three weeks. You will also receive a lapel pin and a credit card-sized credential that shows you are A+ certified shown in Fig. 1-4.

Figure 1-4

The A+ certification card and lapel pin. CompTIA

You will also be able to add the A+ logo to your business cards, though guidelines apply to the logo's size and location. And your employer will receive additional details about using the A+ certification name and logo as a marketing feature. The rules for doing so are presented in Appendix E.

If you do not pass the exam, you can register to take the exam again. But remember that the core and specialty exams must be taken within 90 days of each other.

Once you earn your A+ certification, your status in the IT skills marketplace increases. A+ carries important proof of skills to you the certificate holder and to your customers, your employer, and potential future employers. Understanding the value of your certification will help you use it to the greatest advantage in your career. Chapter 2 explains why, as a certified professional, you are of distinctly greater worth to employers and to the IT industry as a whole.

2

The value of
your certification

C ERTIFICATION benefits everyone in the information technology industry. Understanding its worth to those who employ IT technicians will help you use your certification to its greatest advantage wherever you work. This chapter looks at the benefits of certification in general and then the particular benefits of A+ certification from the perspectives of the technician, the vendor, the reseller, end-user organizations, and industry associations. This chapter emphasizes the value of the A+ certification program. For further information about the value of certification in general, including recent research findings, see Appendix G.

Certification from the IT professional perspective

Certification programs validate your knowledge or skill. They show the marketplace that you have the skill and knowledge to perform a particular job.

The IT industry has been among the most enthusiastic in embracing certification. Increasingly, the value of certification is recognized by IT employers, and the credential can be a passport to better jobs or promotions with your current employer. Certified IT professionals are also often rewarded with higher salaries.

But employers aren't the only ones who believe in the value of certification. As customers increasingly recognize the value of certified IT professionals, they prefer those professionals over their uncertified competitors. After all, in a world of rapidly changing technology, certification may be among the best reasons to believe that a computer professional really can get the job done.

And certification provides a variety of benefits to professionals beyond just landing a job or bringing in new business. For example, the certification process seems to provide professionals with enhanced self-esteem. Some believe that the sense of accomplishment is the greatest reward of attaining a certification. Objective testing and measurement also build confidence by giving a powerful feedback on skills. Those who have been certified have a greater appreciation for

their own skills and how those skills make them a valuable part of the information technology industry.

Certification is often said to give IT professionals more confidence in the interviewing process and more weight in the review process. When cutback or reorganization time comes around, some also find that certification is the lifejacket keeping them afloat.

Driven, in part, by the interest of IT professionals in certification, the number of certification testing programs has grown rapidly in the information technology industry within the past six years. Today, over 40 leading industry vendors and their customers use certification results to help manage their businesses. Vendors and many industry associations offer a wide range of exams, testing fundamental technical skills as well as product-specific knowledge. The exams test skills in networking technologies, operating systems, client/server, databases, developmental tools, and many applications. The IT certifications in the marketplace represent eleven professions common to the industry, including network administrator, network engineer, service technician, instructor, sales representative, office personnel, applications specialist, applications developers, systems administrators, systems operators, and systems engineers.

The growth figures of Sylvan Prometric, the largest developer of certification examinations for the information technology industry, show well the rapid growth of interest in certification. Figure 2-1 illustrates the growing number of programs administered by Sylvan from 1989–1994.

Figure 2-2 shows the growth of Sylvan's testing programs by the technology tested, from first quarter '93 to first quarter '94. The technologies represented include applications development, applications, client/server, network, operating systems, and UNIX.

Certification from the perspective of industry associations

Several organizations address the issues of accountability and professionalism. These organizations are bringing together vendors,

Figure 2-1

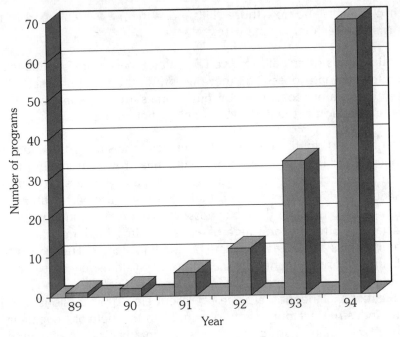

Certification program growth from 1989 to 1994. Sylvan Prometric

Figure 2-2

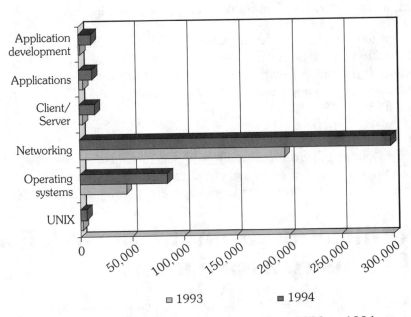

Certification testing growth in seven areas from 1993 to 1994. Sylvan Prometric

resellers, and end users to pool their knowledge and collectively develop standards, courses, and—in some cases—certification programs that advance the interests of the profession as a whole. While vendor-driven certification has led the way over the past five years—industry-driven certification—represented by these programs, is playing an increasingly important role in the certification of IT professionals.

Open Users Recommended Solutions (OURS)

OURS is a not-for-profit group working with end users, vendors, and service providers to help the information technology industry handle challenges in managing and improving multivendor environments.

Its members include vendors like Microsoft, IBM, Novell, and Motorola. Also included are systems integrators, consultants, and major consumers of information technology products and services such as Chase Manhattan Bank, Texaco, and PG&E.

Members gather to consolidate information and offer opinions on key issues and recommend solutions for the industry. The group gives special attention to issues of transition to client/server computing architectures.

In July, 1993, the organization delivered the results of a major study called "Changing I.S. Organizations: The Effect of Client/Server Implementation on Job Skills Requirements." OURS is also delivering a study on object technology in 1995.

OURS can be reached at 312-527-6782.

The Certified Network Expert program

Network General Corporation and Hewlett-Packard Company joined with other companies in the network protocols analyzer marketplace

to address the needs of managers in dealing with the broad spectrum of networking technologies.

In 1993, the group announced a certification program called Certified Network Expert (CNX). The CNX program identifies individuals experienced and knowledgeable in managing, designing, troubleshooting, and maintaining sophisticated multi-vendor networks. Certification is available in four technology areas: Ethernet, token ring, FDDI data link topologies, and LAN cabling. The program does not test for product-specific expertise. CNX testing is available worldwide.

Sponsoring vendors currently include Network General, Hewlett-Packard, IBM, Wandel & Goltermann, The AG Group, MicroTest, Azure Technologies, and Pine Mountain Group.

For more information about the program, call 1-800-CNX-EXAM or 1-612-896-7000.

 # The Institute for Certification of Computer Professionals

Founded in 1973, the ICCP was the original organization to certify computing knowledge and skills. Together with over 20 constituent and affiliate societies, the ICCP represents more than 250,000 IT practitioners; nearly 50,000 have been awarded the certification.

To earn the Certified Computing Professional (CCP) designation today, an applicant needs to satisfy professional experience requirements and pass an exam. Four years of professional computing experience are normally required before sitting for the exam, though educational achievements can account for two of the four years.

The ICCP Core exam consists of sections on human and organization framework, systems concepts, data and information, system development, technology, and associated disciplines. Candidates also must pass two additional exams chosen from ten specialty areas. The ICCP believes that its exams go beyond vendor-specific tests because they assess technical, management, and interpersonal skills.

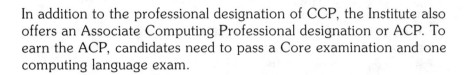

In addition to the professional designation of CCP, the Institute also offers an Associate Computing Professional designation or ACP. To earn the ACP, candidates need to pass a Core examination and one computing language exam.

ICCP also believes in the value of keeping skills up-to-date and requires certificate holders to recertify by completing a minimum of 120 hours of continuing education requirements every three years. The Institute offers self-assessment exams to help certificate holders identify developmental needs and design continuing education plans. (Proficiency certificates can also be earned in any of the specialty or language exams offered.) Recertification can be earned through university courses, vendor courses, authorship, self-study, and other means.

The ICCP is also interested in ensuring the ethical practices of IT professionals. So it requires its certificate holders to commit themselves to the ICCP Code of Ethics and Standard of Conduct. Along with product vendors, the ICCP believes that IT industry self-regulation is preferable to state-enforced licensing. Its programs strive to protect both the public interest and the interest of IT professionals in a way that makes licensing unnecessary.

The ICCP can be reached at 708-299-4227.

The value of A+ certification

A+ from the perspective of industry supporters

Support for the A+ program comes from all corners of the industry and is growing steadily. Original Cornerstone Funding Partners included, among others, industry giants like Apple, Compaq, Hewlett-Packard, Toshiba, and Packard Bell, along with the industry's major service organization, the Association for Field Service Management International. That group has been joined by 27 other financial contributors since January, 1994. (See Appendix A for a complete list of program sponsors.)

Sponsoring companies hope the program will give them an important competitive advantage so they have contributed not only knowledge and cash, but have also jump-started the program by requiring their own employees to be A+ certified. For example, as of October, 1995, Digital Equipment Corporation had 2,022 A+ certified technicians, Bull Information Systems employed 692, Entex had 592, Ingram Micro had 550, Packard Bell had 967, and Technology Service Solutions had 1,169. Several other companies count hundreds of A+ certified technicians on their payrolls.

Packard Bell makes A+ certification a condition of employment for all new service employees, giving them 90 days to become certified after employment. Wang Laboratories requires A+ of all its engineers with PC-support responsibilities.

Ernie Raymond, President of the Permond Solutions Group, Inc., says that for them, "the key selling point for A+ certification is that the first sponsors should have a tremendous edge. They can challenge their competitors on the breadth and depth of their capability to service customers effectively."

Permond considers itself an important A+ supporter. The company was working on its own plan for cross-platform training in a joint venture with vendors when it became aware of CompTIA's plans for A+. Permond joined its program with A+ and began designing its training programs to meet A+ certification requirements.

Many organizations employing A+ certified technicians are also taking advantage of a new program designation: the A+ Authorized Service Center, by ensuring that at least half their service professionals are certified. As of October, 1995, 1,182 service centers were A+ Authorized Service Centers. The number of authorized centers is growing rapidly.

A+ from the perspective of the technician

While A+ growth has been promoted by the IT industry's leading companies, it owes just as much to the enthusiasm of individual technicians. There are many reasons for their enthusiasm.

Don Hurd, a senior field engineer for VanStar, says that A+ material gives "a broad view of what's out there." For Hurd, much of the Macintosh OS-based material was new. Learning it gave him a broader background which he has found useful in his work. The exam, he believes, really covers the bases of the knowledge needed to be successful as a technician today. "If you pass it," he says, "you're thoroughly prepared."

Kenneth Conn, a service technician for Data Source/Connecting Point, says the preparation is especially important for new technicians. "A+ is a base starting point. Preparing for it helps new technicians cement the basics in their minds and helps them feel confident to go out to the customer's site."

Greg Dodge, a senior system engineer for Dataflex, believes that technicians today need to have some knowledge of many things as well as in-depth knowledge of a few. Like Don Hurd, he believes the A+ exam helps technicians learn a great range of general knowledge, including skills in troubleshooting and customer interaction. He says, "With A+, you don't just get people who know a few things and can talk the rest of it. People who've passed the A+ exam have a broad range of knowledge and skill."

Dodge believes that A+ is becoming a kind of requirement to do the job of the technician, or "a ticket to show up for the game." When Dodge goes for hardware training these days, he often encounters one question from the vendor: "Are you A+ certified?" The training requirements, he finds, are often fewer for him as an A+ technician.

Dodge has seen the program's growth in influence first-hand. As one of the early A+ test takers, Dodge says he intended to give his career a boost by adding a credential to his business card. Within months, though, he found that the area competitors were all doing the same. A+ certification was getting attention from area resellers, and soon also from customers who came asking for certified technicians. Today, Dodge's employer—Dataflex—requires their technicians to be A+ certified within 90 days of hire, and one of their chief competitors in their geographic area does also. Dodge believes that A+ is becoming to computer technicians what the CPA is to accountants.

Like accountants facing the CPA exam, technicians often find the A+ exam challenging. For example, Mark Romanowski of U.S. Computer Group is surprised that many people who consider themselves experts are really challenged by A+. Romanowksi praises the real-world quality of the test, especially its testing of customer interaction skills which, he says, "are 70–80% of what technicians do."

David Duanne, a senior engineer for VanStar, agrees. He says the A+ exam is a competency exam, not just a test of book learning or theoretical knowledge. He believes it's difficult to do well on the exam without some field experience to your credit.

Kenneth Conn of Data Source/Connecting Point says, "A+ is not just a paper certification; it reflects a working knowledge of computers. Other certifications are more theoretical, but A+ is a real-world test of skill. You need some experience on the job to pass it."

On the other hand, those technicians who do pass the exam coming right out of school often find that the certification is viewed by some employers as a substitute for experience. Mike Beach, an operations manager at Datasource/Connecting Point, says, "People with strong skills as shown by exams like the A+ exam and who have a very healthy work ethic are in demand even if they don't yet have job experience."

Because of the effectiveness of A+ in measuring the skills needed in the market, having the certification is a great advantage when job-hunting. Peter Sizemore, a systems engineer for Micro Star Co., Inc., says, "During most of the interviews I had—and I had quite a number—they offered me a job because of my A+ certification. A+ is increasingly becoming a necessity."

Ben Eckart, an instructor at the Manhattan-area technical center in Kansas, says that A+ certification has opened new doors for his students even after they have landed a job. For example, one of his students applied to a company that had no interest in the A+ certification program. They hired him, but for other reasons. Within a few months, however, the company was so sold on the A+ program that they stopped providing training to any of their employees who weren't A+ certified.

Eckart has always encouraged his students to pursue A+ certification even before they find work. He says his students were not all convinced of the value of A+ certification, but they are finding with A+ that they are getting better jobs and advancing more quickly. Eckart says, "Whether you personally believe in the value of certification or not, you'll find that you need to be certified today to get ahead."

Because of the recognition given the credential, being A+ certified often increases a technician's level of self-assurance. Kenneth Conn says, "Anyone in any line of work needs to feel value, needs to understand how they fit into the group that is their peers. A+ gives you that sense of value. When you have it, you feel more confident of your abilities." John Hlavac of Packard-Bell says, "By being A+ certified, there is an extra level of job satisfaction and personal satisfaction, of confidence in abilities and skills—and recognition for it."

Bill York, a past co-chair of the A+ Advisory Committee, says that the A+ program "is a step higher than certification on particular products because it is recognized throughout the industry." York reports that his own technicians at SolutioNetics embrace the program enthusiastically. "All of my technicians are standing in line," he says, "so they can prove their value to me and to their peers and clients."

 # A+ from the vendor perspective

Among the chief benefits of A+ certification for vendors is that it provides a way to ensure quality of their product resellers. Gary Turner, Director of North American Service Operations at Exide Electronics in Raleigh, NC, says that A+ certification is part of a strategic decision Exide made to become partners with their value-added resellers rather than just suppliers. "With A+ certification, we can help them grow their business, which of course strengthens the channel by taking our products to our customers."

At the same time, A+ helps vendors to reduce training costs. Many hardware vendors are saving time and money by relying on A+ certification training to cover "the basics." The vendor no longer has to teach the fundamentals of laser printers or color displays when their

classes consist of A+ certified technicians. This allows vendors to spend training time on the features that differentiate their products.

Mary Pizzo, National Support Services Manager at Apple, says, "The A+ program is critical to both Apple and to our service providers. It allows our service providers to reduce training time while increasing productivity for their service technicians. Knowing our service providers are A+ certified, in turn, allows Apple to focus our training on meeting the specific needs of our customers."

Some hardware vendors are shortening their training programs as a result. Bill York, former co-chair of the A+ Advisory Committee, reported shortening of at least some training classes at Packard Bell, Apple, IBM, Toshiba, Hewlett-Packard, and Epson. "This means a technician spends less time in class and gets back on the job sooner," York said.

But not all vendor training programs are getting shorter as a result. For example, while Compaq Computer Corp. is removing modules from training courses wherever the material is covered by A+ certification, it is also including more products in its courses and giving more training and hands-on time, something that Compaq can advertise as a benefit to the consumer.

A+ certification also helps vendors prepare their own in-house technicians to be successful. For example, Tom Brooks, Manager of Technical Training for AST Research, says that while AST doesn't require A+ certification of its resellers, it does strongly encourage it for all of its phone and field technicians. A+ certification minimizes the training needed once a technician is hired and lets the technician focus on learning AST's own technologies.

A+ requirements strengthen the level of confidence that vendors have in their technicians. Don Jones, technologist for Microsoft North America, says that with A+, "We can put a new person in front of a customer without being terrified. We won't hire technicians without it."

With the certification as a hiring guideline, the hiring process can be much shorter. Don Jones says, "With A+ certification, there is a lot less screening needed. We no longer have to conduct three interviews for each potential new hire. We now can get by with just one."

A+ is also helpful with planning for internal training and promotions. As Don Jones says, "because of the way A+ certification test results are reported back to us, I can see the areas where my people need further training."

Packard Bell is one manufacturer that has chosen to require A+ both for the field technicians supporting its products and for its in-house technical support staff. David McWilliams, Training Manager of Packard Bell's service and support group, says that requiring A+ of outside service providers guarantees a higher skill set for them as well as a more positive response by the end user.

At the same time, requiring A+ of its internal technical support staff means that Packard Bell has a standard against which to compare the skills of those technicians, and therefore a way to keep their quality high. McWilliams also values the way the exam focuses the attention of those preparing for it. For test candidates from Packard Bell, it means passing the Microsoft Windows/DOS specialty exam, which includes knowledge fundamental to work with Packard Bell systems.

 # A+ from the reseller perspective

Many resellers report that certification allows them to promote themselves on quality of service, and thereby build solid relationships, which are the basis of their success.

For winning new business, the certification may well continue to grow in importance as customers, including government, increasingly appreciate its importance. Some believe that the certification will soon be required in government requests for proposal (RFPs).

Tom Henninger, business planning manager for Wang Laboratories' Worldwide Customer Service Organization, believes that the certification is already implied in RFPs he's dealt with. "Frequently an RFP requires that service technicians be certified by the vendors on whose equipment they work. A+ certification meets this requirement," Henninger says.

The A+ program is now listed in the *Guide to National Professional Certification Programs*, a book used by government agencies, their contractors, and private sector human resource departments.

In addition to bolstering consumer confidence, A+ certification strengthens the channel in another important way: it significantly reduces costs. Costs for service at all levels—end user, reseller, and manufacturer—have been skyrocketing in recent years. An important component of those costs has been the training expense to bring sales and service representatives up to speed on the variety of new products entering the marketplace. Through A+ certification, training costs are significantly lowered.

A manager at a major reseller praises A+ for helping them to avoid redundant costs. "I have to be authorized on all of the different manufacturers' products," he says. "To do that, I have to spend a lot of time and money to go to all of the different training events across the country. The cost of training and travel and time away from the job is very critical to us. The A+ program allows us to eliminate the base level of training. Then we can concentrate on learning the specific technology required by the different manufacturers."

Tracy Ligon agrees. While Senior Director of Service Operations for Tandy, Ligon wrestled with training requirements imposed by approximately 50 of the 90 manufacturers with whom Tandy did business. When those 50 manufacturers each required service technicians to take basic training, the total training cost to Tandy was "outrageous," Ligon says. But today, when those same manufacturers accept the A+ certification as satisfying their basic training requirements, the training burden has fallen by about one day per technician per manufacturer. This saves Tandy approximately one week of training per year for each of their 1,600 technicians.

As an independent consultant today, Ligon advises his clients, both resellers and end-user organizations, to have their technical staffs A+ certified.

Lex Darr, a service manager at VanStar, says that A+ is helpful to him as a hiring manager. Without A+ certification as a guide in hiring, he says, hiring good service people is sometimes a matter of luck. But, he says, certification results, "don't lie like resumes sometimes do." Darr also believes that A+ certification is much more useful information to a manager than a certificate from a vendor-sponsored training program. Technicians may receive the course certificate, he says, whether they learned anything or not. The A+ certificate, in contrast, shows that technicians have the knowledge to produce results.

Tim Fell, a service manager for InaCom Information, says that InaCom requires A+ certification for all of their technicians. He says that it satisfies the base level training requirements of many of their manufacturers and also serves as a stepping stone in the natural career progress of technicians. Technicians, he says, progress from the A+ certified basics into more product-specific knowledge as they develop. He likes to have his technicians A+ certified before they branch out into the product lines of several manufacturers or into the networking field.

 # A+ from the customers and end-user organization perspective

As to the program's effects on customer confidence, David Bossi of IBM says that A+ has helped IBM to deliver better service both internally and through their reseller organizations. Service, he says, is a logistics problem. "It's the right personnel with the right part at the right time with the proper professionalism." Professionalism, he believes, can make up for lateness of parts and other logistical problems. And A+, he says, has improved their rating on professionalism.

Bill York says that A+ has improved the satisfaction of customers at SolutioNetics. He says that with the wide product mix they service, A+ helps them to prove they have invested the needed time and effort to give quality service.

Galen Davis says, "At Intel Corporation, we look at A+ certification as a basic literacy test; something that is of primary benefit to our customers rather than to us directly."

Some technicians report that A+ is not yet well known among smaller clients. But the larger accounts know it and require it. David Duanne of VanStar says that Sprint required A+ certification of technicians working on an on-site project. Many of those slated to be on the project went off to become A+ certified in a hurry.

A+ certification has also been embraced by end-user organizations who use A+ as a requirement for their own technical staff. Increasingly, organizations require their own technicians, and even telephone support and sales people, to be A+ certified. Many also structure internal training programs around A+ certification requirements, and use A+ as a useful reference when hiring.

Rick Brown, Manager of Technical Support at Conner Peripherals, comments on the value of A+ to corporate end users. "A+ is a way to quantify the basic set of skills needed to exist in the technical workplace. For technicians, it's a way of saying 'This is what I bring to the table.' From the perspective of reseller and corporate managers, it has been hard to quantify the skills needed for field service and help desk professionals. A+ has helped define those skills and show who really has them. Once you know that your technicians have the core technical skills, you can begin to invest in working with them on the finer, soft skills that make for good customer relations."

A+ and industry self-regulation

The A+ program serves a variety of needs common to the IT industry, not least of which may be strengthening industry self-regulation in a way that avoids government controls. Nathan Morton, former CEO of CompUSA, says that the A+ program has established important "self-policing" mechanisms for the industry.

A CompTIA representative says, "Several states have already proposed legislation that would regulate the information technology industry. A self-regulating industry that certifies its members with a program like A+ can minimize such government-imposed efforts."

The changing market for information technology skills

THIS chapter documents the rapidly changing skill sets required of IT technicians and the technician's need for training and development, and for certification. It will give you a sense of the skills that will be useful to your professional development in a variety of IT work environments.

The chapter also gives an overview of the IT product distribution and service chain, identifying the major employment areas for service technicians. The chapter concludes with career advice from three experts who know both the market for IT services and the A+ exam.

A changing market for skills

Robert Half International, in its recent salary guide, reports that "the hiring outlook in the information technology employment area is bright. The need for professionals who can design and implement advanced systems will remain strong as companies of all sizes continue investing more freely in technology.

"Nationally, companies are reporting demand for microcomputer programmers, programmer analysts, and systems administrators." (Robert Half International, Inc.) Robert Half also finds firms investing in network technology in record numbers, resulting in very strong demand for administrators and engineers who specialize in Local Area Network and Wide Area Network environments.

In regions with a shortage of these experts, firms are paying higher salaries and, in many cases, at least a portion of relocation costs for top candidates. The demand for networking skills is predicted to grow.

The U.S. Department of Labor also sees a bright future for information technology skills. It considers computing the nation's second fastest-growing industry, with a projected annual growth rate of 4.4 percent through the year 2005.

The IT industry as a whole is very healthy, and so is that subset of the IT industry in which computer technicians most commonly work: the microcomputer market. For example, in 1993, United States personal

computer industry revenues were over $66 billion, not including sales of work stations. In 1994, 18.6 million personal computers were sold in the United States.

In the growing IT and microcomputer industries, service is increasingly becoming a crucial source of profits, more important than hardware sales. Service is important for all phases of activity in which computer technicians will find themselves working in the coming years, including computer maintenance and work with system software and networking.

The research firm Dataquest predicted in December, 1993 that the overall hardware maintenance market in the U.S. would grow at a combined annual growth rate of 8.5% through 1997. At the same time, Dataquest identified software-related service and value-added service opportunities as being the faster growing areas of service revenues.

Customer reliance on service and support for hardware, software, and related areas will continue to grow. For example, today's users must determine if they need a PC or a workstation, which operating system to use, and whether to buy custom programming or off-the-shelf software to fit their needs. They must also determine which network, protocol, and corresponding cables they need for their Local Area Network and Wide Area Network. Customers need quality advice and consulting as well as quality service and support for increasingly complex products.

Dataquest found that customers identify a wide variety of technologies for which they need support and training. Client/server architecture and Local Area Network integration are two of the most important areas. See Figs. 3-1 and 3-2.

With new technologies flooding the market, the IT education and training market is flourishing, including among its customers both computer professionals as well as end users. The technical skills training in highest demand are shown in Fig. 3-3.

Figure 3-4 shows Dataquest's projections for the potential dollars that corporate clients will spend on outside IT education and training services; amounts budgeted for internally provided services are not included.

Figure 3-1

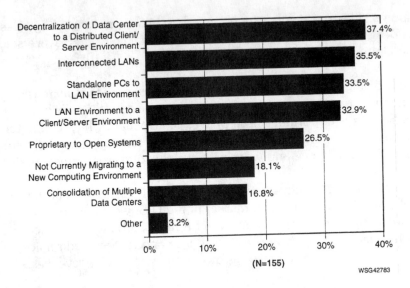

Recent or expected changes in respondents' computing environment. Dataquest, 1995

Figure 3-2

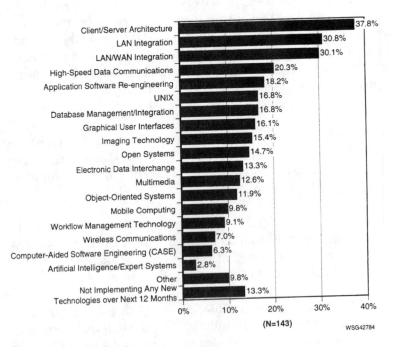

Technologies to be implemented over the next twelve months.
Dataquest, 1995

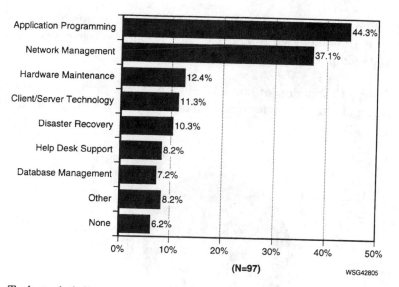

Figure 3-3

Technical skill training currently in highest demand. Dataquest, 1995

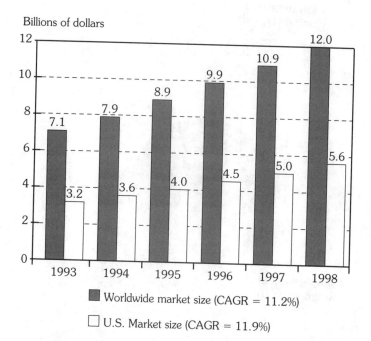

Figure 3-4

IT education and training forecast. Dataquest, 1995

The portion of those training dollars in the United States by service segment is shown below. Networking and desktop services will grow while Data Center services shrink. (See Fig. 3-5.)

The projected allocation of budget to technical recipients shows that the portion allotted to system managers and applications programmers

Figure 3-5

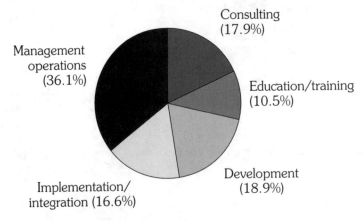

1994 Total = $75,547 million

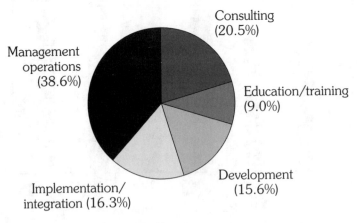

1998 Total = $133,511 million

U.S. education and training market forecast by the service segment. Dataquest, 1995

will decline while the portion allotted for end-user support will increase. (See Fig. 3-6.)

In the multiproduct environment, cross-product training and "soft skills" training are expected to grow faster than product-specific course offerings. Soft skills include such things as management and people

Figure 3-6

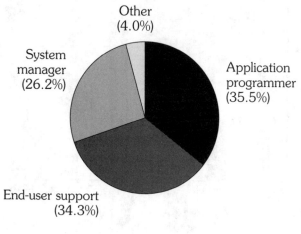

Other
(4.0%)

System
manager
(26.2%)

Application
programmer
(35.5%)

End-user support
(34.3%)

1994 (N = 65)

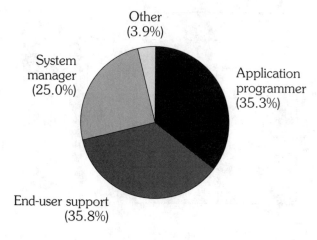

Other
(3.9%)

System
manager
(25.0%)

Application
programmer
(35.3%)

End-user support
(35.8%)

1996 (N = 65)

Technical recipients of IT budget allocation. Dataquest, 1995

skills as well as time management. Cross-product training is technical in nature, but not product-specific. Cross-product skills and soft skills will be important both to end users and to technicians. (See Fig. 3-7.)

Figure 3-7

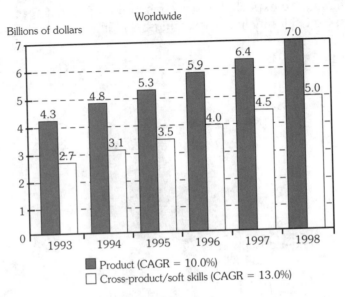

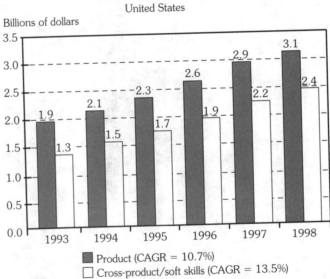

Customer needs for product and cross-product/soft-skills training continue to grow. Dataquest, 1995

The Dataquest study documents the rapidly changing technical environment in which both end users and computer professionals work. It highlights the need for continuous training and the need for training in areas that can be called "cross-product."

The organization Open Users Recommended Solutions (OURS) reached similar conclusions in a study performed with the Gartner Group in 1993. The study surveyed 150 information technology (IT) professionals from a variety of job roles including executives, front-line managers, and staff. Respondents represented a variety of organizations including banks, insurance companies, manufacturers, service providers, and state and local government agencies. The study also drew from the Gartner Group's survey of 15,000 IT professionals.

The results point to a dramatic shift in the roles and responsibilities of computing professionals. They strongly suggest a need for training and for the certification of skills. Here are some of the key findings of the study for five areas of operation:

Data center operation

IT departments will be changing their skills along with their tools to better exploit advanced technologies. For example, the new corporate environments are both smaller and more "open," in the sense that computing is no longer an isolated function but one that connects every worker in the enterprise. IT professionals within the corporation need to become more responsive and service-oriented, able to deliver the solutions their corporate users require.

At the same time, respondents to the survey expect that the importance and complexity of networks will soon force their companies to consolidate data centers with the Local Area Network (LAN) and Wide Area Network (WAN) groups.

Data center managers see themselves as increasingly responsible for LAN, WAN, and data processing simultaneously. They believe these services will not be provided through traditional mainframe technologies, but more often through server operating systems such as UNIX and Microsoft's Windows NT. To support the transition, OURS

concludes that the new IT professional will have to be "retrained in programming disciplines, management disciplines, and the tools that will enable this new architecture."

The top skills that respondents felt they would need in the data center of the future are:

➤ UNIX operating systems and systems programming

➤ Capacity planning in distributed environments

➤ Host and server scheduling procedures

➤ Disaster recovery and backup for PCs

➤ Graphical user interfaces and artificial intelligence for automated operations

Applications development

Respondents to the survey predicted a change in job roles for applications developers between 1993 and 1997. For example, programmers are increasingly able to program through pictures, icons, and objects. In essence, the system generates the code. This rise of "computer-aided software engineering" will decrease the programmer's need to code and test, while increasing his or her need to understand the business; plan, analyze, and design software; and measure the results in productivity.

LAN operations

LAN administrators expect to be increasingly viewed as "mission-critical." The LAN is the first layer of access into the corporate computing hierarchy and will need the same level of integrity, security, recoverability, and scalability offered on today's mainframes. To accomplish this, LAN professionals will need new technical abilities along with management skills.

Respondents expect to spend less time on rote, labor-intensive functions such as adds, moves, and changes. They expect to spend more time on strategy including measuring performance; handling software distribution; and managing applications, disaster recovery, and security.

The top skills needed to support the LAN environment will be:

➤ LAN process/traffic flow analysis

➤ Directory services maintenance

➤ PC and network operating systems skills

WAN operations

Those working with WAN communications will need to learn a variety of skills for working with client/server, internetwork, and LAN technologies. At the same time, like the LAN professional, the WAN operator will rise in strategic perspective.

For example, new technologies such as Asynchronous Transfer Mode (ATM) and Switched Multimegabit Data Service (SMDS) will compel WAN managers to rethink the sources of their services, the designs of their networks, and the financial impact of redesigning their WANs. In the future, they will be less concerned with ordering bandwidth and more concerned with understanding the applications requirements of the business.

The top skills in this area will include:

➤ Negotiation

➤ Network management tools

➤ Business project management

Architecture and planning

Systems architects of the near future will need to create "non-technical" systems to better communicate with users. They will need to build systems that work easily and promote productivity.

Among the top skills needed in this area will be:

➤ Business modeling

➤ Technology transfer

➤ Migration planning

47

According to OURS, "The technology shift is undeniable and unstoppable, and many of the new technologies that will comprise these new applications will be new to IT organizations. With these innovations, IT organizations will need to retrain their existing staff and seek new employees with skill sets that are currently in rare supply."

Respondents said they see their skill retraining needs increasing, but 49% did not expect their company's budget to expand to meet this need. Most also felt that their company's training plans were focused on product training rather than training in process and concepts.

The report cautioned that failure to train properly for the future may lead to serious consequences, including failure to assimilate the new technologies, unproductive users and IT professionals, and a falloff in productivity.

The connection of certification with productivity was documented in an October, 1995 study by the International Data Corporation called "The Financial Benefits of Certification." The study focused exclusively on internal corporate IT departments in client/server environments and drew input from 253 IT managers and directors.

The study compared the efficiency and effectiveness of organizations that embrace certification with those that do not. Certification supporters were defined as those who pay for or otherwise support employees' becoming professionally certified and/or require professional certification when hiring IT employees. In the study sample, certification-supporting companies had about three times the proportion of staff certified than did nonsupporting companies.

The study found that:

> ➤ Certification supporters operate more sophisticated client/server environments than those companies that do not support certification.

> ➤ The productivity of IT staff in companies that support certification is greater than that of companies that do not support certification.

> ➤ The payback time on investments in certification is typically less than nine months.

Some of their results are shown later.

Results suggested that certification helped companies make greater use of new technologies. Figure 3-8 shows that companies supporting certification tend to be much more decentralized than those that do not. Figure 3-9 shows that companies supporting certification are supporting more advanced desktop operating environments.

Figure 3-8

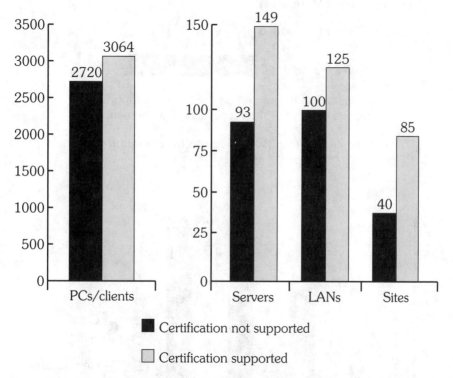

■ Certification not supported

□ Certification supported

Average number of sites, LANs, servers, and PCs. International Data Corporation

Certification supporters seemed to accomplish more with technology without employing larger staffs; their staffs were not larger, but were more productive. Figure 3-10 shows that, in the certification supporting companies, support for the more decentralized environment did not require a greater number of IT staff. Figure 3-11 shows that IT employees at certification advocates' sites handle more support calls per employee per day. Figure 3-12 shows that

Figure 3-9

Windows

Certification supported ████████████████ 66%

Certification not supported ██████████ 51%

DOS (without Windows)

Certification supported ████ 10%

Certification not supported █████ 15%

Companies that support certification are supporting
more advanced desktop operating environments.

Average percent of clients running specific operating systems.
International Data Corporation

Figure 3-10

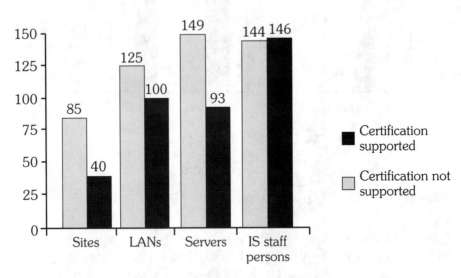

In the certification supporting companies, support for the more
decentralized environment did not require a greater number of IS
staff. Average IS staff was the same for both company types.

Average number of LANs, servers, and sites supported by an IT staff.
International Data Corporation

Figure 3-11

	Average no. of sites	Avg. daily support calls per IS employee	No. of PCs connected to LANs	No. of servers
Advocates	67	21	4142	167
Nonbelievers	47	15	2617	97

IS employees at certification advocates' sites handle more support calls per employee per day.

Differences in workload between certification advocates and nonbelievers in certification. International Data Corporation

Figure 3-12

	No. of PCs per server	Downtime cost per hour	Avg. downtime per server (hrs.)	Downtime cost per server
Advocates	25	$191	3.5	$669
Nonbelievers	27	$208	5.3	$1,102

Certification advocates report shorter downtimes and lower associated costs than do certification non-believers.

Differences in unscheduled downtime between certification advocates and nonbelievers in certification. International Data Corporation

certification advocates report shorter downtimes and lower associated costs than do certification nonbelievers.

It is not only the certification supporters who view certified employees as more productive. Many of the nonsupporters viewed certified employees as more productive also. Figure 3-13 shows that 78% of companies supporting certification feel that certified employees are more productive in at least their area of certification, while only about half of certification nonsupporters feel that this is the case.

Figure 3-13

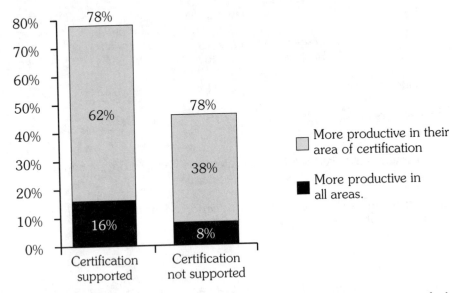

Seventy-eight percent of companies supporting certification feel that certified employees are more productive in at least their area of certification, close to half of certification nonsupporters feel this is the case.

Are certified employees more productive? International Data Corporation

The top five benefits that the sample group expected to receive from certifying employees included:

➤ Providing a greater knowledge and increased productivity

➤ Assuring a certain level of expertise and skill

➤ Improving support quality

➤ Reducing training costs

➤ Providing higher morale and commitment

For the great majority, those benefits of certification were realized. (See Fig. 3-14.)

The technical skills needed to operate productively in the workplace are escalating sharply, pushing demand for training and development, as well as for certification. The value of certification, and of A+ certification in particular, is continually growing.

Were these benefits realized?

Figure 3-14

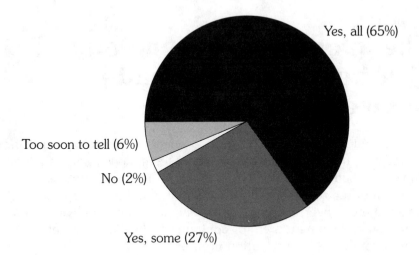

Yes, all (65%)

Too soon to tell (6%)

No (2%)

Yes, some (27%)

Ninety-two percent realized expected benefits from certification.
International Data Corporation

A+ has proven valuable for reducing redundant training and thereby making training dollars go further. It has also focused attention on those areas of skill that are truly cross-product and fundamental, and that can be valuable as a base for learning other specific new technologies as they come on-line.

Finally, in a world of rapidly changing demands on the skills of computer technicians, A+ has focused attention on those skills that all technicians need to have, regardless of the environment they work in. In that way, it has become a useful gauge for technicians in evaluating their current skills and planning their future development.

See Appendix F for the Job Profile of a Computer Technician. This profile, developed by CompTIA, in coordination with dozens of IT industry leaders, identifies the major skills required of service technicians. That profile also identifies some areas of responsibility not currently tested on the A+ exam including business management, administrative skills, and professionalism. Each of these is discussed in Appendix F for its importance in the work of technicians today. Note that customer interaction skills—described in the profile—have been

tested in past versions of the A+ exam, and will probably be tested in forthcoming versions of the exam.

 # The information technology distribution channel and its service requirements

The distribution system for computer products is constantly changing and adapting to requirements imposed by technology and by the end-user. A distribution model is shown in Fig. 3-15, followed by a discussion of the role played by each link in the distribution chain today and the concerns of each for quality service. Each link in the chain is an employment area for computer technicians, and each benefits from the A+ certification program.

Understanding the needs of each of these employers for quality service can help you, as an A+ certified technician, to use your professional

Figure 3-15

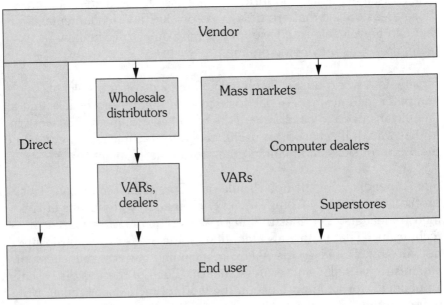

The distribution model. Dataquest, 1995

skills to your greatest advantage, both in finding jobs and in serving well in the jobs you take. For materials on job networking, interviewing, and resumes, see the book list provided in Appendix C.

A customer may purchase a computer from a variety of sources. The collective group of all sources is called the distribution channel. Examples of purchasing possibilities are direct sale from the manufacturer (also called the vendor), sales from computer stores, value-added resellers (VARs), and mail order. (See Fig. 3-15.)

Value-added resellers and computer dealers, in turn, may receive their products directly from the vendor or through distributors or aggregators.

 # The manufacturer as a service provider

When corporations need to make a large purchase of IT equipment, they may try to negotiate a sale at discount directly from the manufacturer. A corporate buyer may also ask the manufacturer to reconfigure personal computers in order to meet custom requirements for hardware or software configuration.

Some corporate buyers prefer direct purchases not just for the savings and chance to have products customized but also because they want to receive service and support directly from the manufacturer. In recent years, some vendors have encouraged this by publishing their own catalogs and marketing themselves more aggressively to end users.

The computer manufacturer determines the warranty period and guidelines for service of their products. The manufacturer may provide all warranty service or authorize other service providers, including dealers, to handle warranty work. Either way, it is important to the manufacturer that the warranty work be done completely and accurately. When the manufacturer provides service itself, it may either require that the product be sent to it, or it may send service technicians to the customer's site.

A manufacturer's warranty may cover the complete costs for certain kinds of repairs. Other repairs may require the customer to pay for the costs of repair time and materials.

Both manufacturers and resellers are working to reduce costs through better management of parts inventory and other overhead costs. Manufacturers are also designing hardware systems to be more easily serviced.

At the same time, both manufacturers and resellers are abandoning the old view of service as a cost of doing business, and looking at service as a major revenue opportunity. This new view is taking them beyond merely servicing and maintaining hardware into servicing software and providing a range of professional services including software integration (SI), network integration, facilities management, help desk support, and education and training. That transition is shown in Fig. 3-16.

Many manufacturers are planning to increase opportunities to earn service revenues by building customer loyalty through extended warranty periods and the bundling of more free warranty support and service into the product purchase.

At the same time, in order to provide the new services, many manufacturers and service providers are investing in employee training to give them the skills they need.

Service technicians working for manufacturers will play an increasing number of roles. They will continue to provide board or component repair to end users as well as troubleshooting support to technicians in reseller organizations, but increasingly, they will also serve as help-desk support, trainers and educators, and providers of networking and software integration support.

Resellers as service providers

The reseller channels are responsible for ensuring ongoing service and support for the products they represent. Most resellers employ their

Figure 3-16

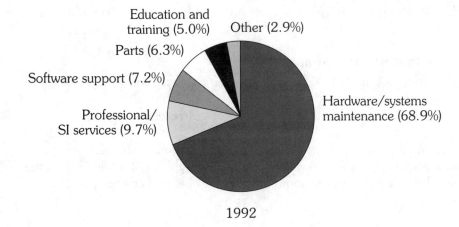

1992

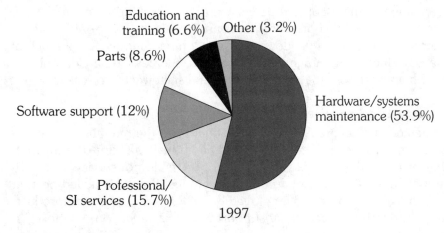

1997

Vendor service revenue composition. Dataquest, 1995

own technicians, although some may contract with a servicing company for them.

Technicians working for resellers are typically responsible for all the product brands sold. They provide warranty service and may perform all of the key tasks and duties listed in the A+ service technician job profile. Resellers service customers either through a "depot" or service desk in the reseller's location or by having the technician travel to the customer location to provide on-site service.

Below are listed the various components of the reseller distribution network.

✳ **Distributors/aggregators**

Distributors handle large inventories of products and many different brands, and can provide cost-effective distribution help to manufacturers who sell to multiple types of resellers and VARs.

Often, distributors offer service support for their customers and warranty support for manufacturers. They typically handle both small and large-volume sales; some sell through catalogs directly to end users.

Aggregators, in contrast, sell only to large reseller organizations, and pass along to them considerable savings based on large volume purchases. Examples of aggregators are Intelligent Electronics and MicroAge, Inc. Some vendors, such as Compaq and IBM, sell much of their product through aggregators; others, such as Apple Computer, Inc., have tried to bypass aggregators and sell directly to resellers.

✳ **Value-added resellers**

Value-added resellers (VARs) buy product from the manufacturer or from wholesale distributors, then add additional software or hardware that provides the "added value." Often, VARs do not service and support the manufacturers' hardware, but just the value-added portion of their sale. Technicians employed by VARs must learn their products in great depth to successfully support customized versions of those products.

✳ **Original equipment manufacturers**

An Original Equipment Manufacturer (OEM) is similar to a value-added reseller. The major difference is that the OEM buys product from a manufacturer, integrates a specific application or change into the product, and sells it under a different name. For example, an OEM may buy monitors from several monitor manufacturers, then make some internal changes and add its logo and company name. OEMs provide all the same kinds of service support to their products that manufacturers do.

✳ Computer stores/dealers

A computer store may be independently owned, a franchise, or part of a national or regional chain. They are often called resellers or "dealers." An individually owned store is a retail business responsible for all aspects of sales, service, and support. Franchised stores are contractually part of a larger computer reseller network. Individual store owners enter into franchise agreements in order to share in larger discount purchases with other stores and to gain other benefits such as national advertising, name recognition, and a larger service support network.

Some computer resellers are regional chains in which several stores in a geographic area are under one ownership. These stores are usually required to have service technicians to provide customer support and installation. The service technicians in regional chains may also provide warranty work on behalf of the computer manufacturer.

✳ Mass markets as service providers

Mass marketers such as Sears, Wal-Mart, and others purchase IT products in large volume and sell in large volume directly to end users. As computer prices drop, the mass market is increasingly important in the distribution chain. Few of the mass marketers service and support the products they sell, and mass market customers often seek service from the product manufacturer.

Mail order and service

Mail order can be a simple and effective way to buy computers when customers need no help from salespeople in making buying decisions, but already know the equipment and applications they need. Generally, mail order products needing repair within the warranty period are shipped back to the mail order house. These repairs are usually made by swapping a new component for the defective one.

Third-party maintenance providers and service

Third-party maintenance providers (TPMs) are usually part of regional chains, and provide service transactions and warranty repair as their primary business. TPMs typically service many brands of computers, peripherals, and related products. Some offer depot service so that customers can mail or drop off computer equipment to them for exchange or repair.

TPMs represent the product manufacturer, and usually the TPM's contact with the customer begins when the customer service call is transferred or dispatched to them from the manufacturer. For example, Apple Computer does not employ servicing technicians for customer support. When customers call Apple Computer's 800 service number, the operator dispatches the call to the servicing agent in the customer's area who acts as Apple's representative.

For most of the organizations in the distribution chain, and certainly for distributors, VARs, OEMs, computer stores, and TPMs, the success of their business comes increasingly from the success of their service. The more maintenance, support, and value-added service they provide, the more successful their businesses will be in the coming years. High quality service technicians who are well trained in the basics and ready to take on new roles for service and support will be of great value to these organizations. For this reason, many of them are encouraging, if not requiring, their technicians to be A+ certified.

Service and the corporate end-user

Large businesses that use many brands of IT equipment and that need immediate service to avoid downtime may set up their own internal service and support organization. Such businesses send their service technician employees to product training seminars sponsored by

vendors and keep key spare parts in their company inventories. In-house service technician jobs can be found in corporations, government, and universities.

But while in-house support makes a company more independent and potentially less subject to downtime, going outside for service helps businesses cut their overhead and provides them the kind of specialized skills needed for their increasingly complex applications. Many companies, of course, use a combination of in-house and external IT support. Dataquest projects that, overall, the proportion of company IT budgets going to internally provided services will increase slightly in the near-term future relative to outside services.

The overall budget allocation for internal and external services for corporate clients is represented below. The internal services budget goes primarily to hardware and software maintenance as well as to daily operations. The external services budget goes primarily to hardware and software maintenance and consulting and advisory services. (See Figs. 3-17 and 3-18.)

As the microcomputer industry continues to grow, the need for quality service technicians grows also. Those with solid technical skills and with an appreciation for the fundamentals of customer satisfaction will add value to their employer, in whatever place their employer holds in the distribution chain.

Developing and certifying a broad range of skills from the A+ fundamentals on up to networking and product-specific expertise will open new opportunities at every turn. Seeking out employers who value the role of training and the need for excellence in customer satisfaction will also keep your career on the fast track.

Some advice from the experts

Below, three IT industry experts offer career advice and perspectives on the credential you are about to earn.

Figure 3-17

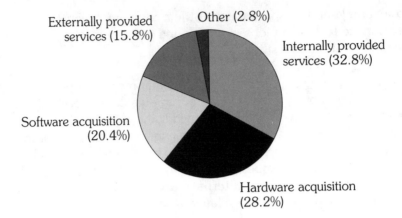

1994 (N = 112)

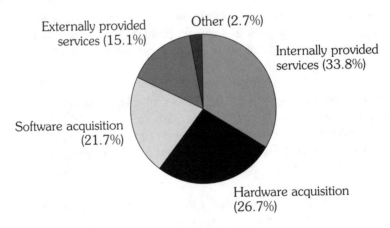

1996 (N = 112)

IT budget allocations, 1994 and 1996. Dataquest, 1995

 # ⇨ Advice to beginner computer technicians

Aaron Woods

**Professional Services Programs and Business Development
Consultant in Parker, Colorado, formerly Director of National
Service Programs and Training with Intelligent Electronics**

Figure 3-18

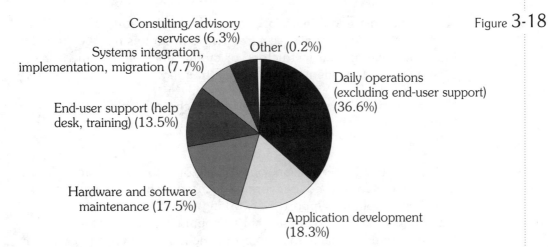

Consulting/advisory services (6.3%)

Systems integration, implementation, migration (7.7%)

Other (0.2%)

Daily operations (excluding end-user support) (36.6%)

End-user support (help desk, training) (13.5%)

Hardware and software maintenance (17.5%)

Application development (18.3%)

Internal services (N = 92)

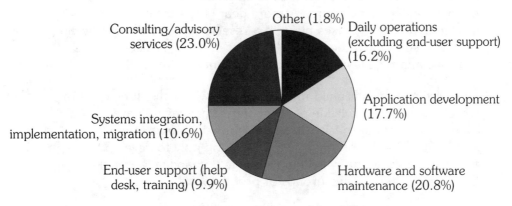

Consulting/advisory services (23.0%)

Other (1.8%)

Daily operations (excluding end-user support) (16.2%)

Application development (17.7%)

Systems integration, implementation, migration (10.6%)

End-user support (help desk, training) (9.9%)

Hardware and software maintenance (20.8%)

External services (N = 92)

1994 internal and external services budget allocation. Dataquest, 1995

"Most technicians today start their training in a technical school or two-year or community college, sometimes springboarding from there into a four-year college degree. People can get a diploma as a computer technician in nine months to two years.

"There are many options, but people really need to do their homework when choosing where to study. The technical institutes can

be very expensive and may not provide the kind of state-of-the-art training that new graduates require. Those programs may be limited by the knowledge of their instructors, or by the kinds of equipment they have available to students for hands-on training.

"I often recommend junior colleges over technical schools because they may provide an excellent computer technician program along with studies in other areas.

"After becoming a technician, one usually opts today for either the networking area or a nonnetworking focused technical support area including telephone support. Networking techs may advance into networking analysis, then into management positions. Those outside the networking specialty may go on to supervise a service department or telephone support group on their way up to management.

"The networking services area is more a professional services area geared toward installing and maintaining complex systems. The nonnetworking services area is more geared toward fixing what is broken and typically takes place in a reseller environment. Providing sales and support to the reseller's clients is often particularly time-sensitive and requires excellent customer interaction skills.

"A+ certification is useful for either of the two tracks. It demonstrates a broad general knowledge of computer principles that are helpful both to networking specialists and to nonnetworking service specialists. The A+ program is also working now to develop an additional module that will help to bridge the language and skills gap that separates these two groups of professionals.

"That gap today is large and frustrating for many. A technician may go out to the client's site to repair a bad drive. The technician repairs and replaces the drive and brings the drive back up, and the unit works fine until it is connected back to the network. At that point, the technician may not have enough knowledge to isolate the problem. The A+ program will soon help on-site technicians to ensure they have the skills they need to at least talk intelligently to network engineers and play a constructive role in resolving such problems.

"The A+ program is dynamic; it will always keep up with the changing needs of the industry as they become evident. A+, as well as certifications provided by the product vendors, will play an increasingly important role for computer technicians, who will inevitably be involved in a life-long learning process."

 # A+ and a suggested skills progression for computer technicians

Mariano Dy-Liacco

Vice President of Service and Support Operations for Dataflex Corporation, Clearwater, Florida

"At Dataflex, we've developed a curriculum of four distinct levels for computer technicians. These steps of progress are useful not only for technicians here; they could be a model for others to follow in developing their careers. The progression is from general knowledge to more specific product-related skills.

"Level One of our curriculum requires technicians to meet the basic training requirements of the manufacturers whose products we work on, including Apple, Compaq, Hewlett-Packard, and IBM. We also require at Level One that all of our technicians earn A+ certification. In fact, they need to earn that credential within 90 days of hire date as a condition of employment. We put together study groups for our A+ people and encouraged them to work together and share study materials.

"The knowledge tested by A+ is the solid basis on which other, more specific components of knowledge and skill can be built. A+ has been essential for our industry in identifying those fundamentals and so helping to chart career progress for computer technicians.

"Level Two of our curriculum has our technicians focus on software, including operating systems and applications programs. In the mid-1980s, 80% of what a technician had to know was hardware-related, while only 20% was software-related. Today, those percentages are reversed. Because hardware systems have become more modular and easier to repair while software programs have proliferated and become more complex, technicians need to focus most of their energies on learning the software side. At Level Two, our technicians learn such

software as Microsoft programs and OS/2, and take electives such as Excel, Word, and others.

"Level Three requires our technicians to develop deeper knowledge about both hardware and software and to learn some networking skills. The best technicians have all of these skills well developed.

"Our fourth level is a particular product specialization, which technicians choose for themselves.

"I would recommend something like these four steps of progression for every technician. But the exact direction of the specialization will differ from one technician to another, and appropriate directions of specialization will change constantly as the marketplace changes.

"Technicians need to watch the trends. You don't want to specialize in one kind of technology when the trends are all pointing to another. In every case, though, training for technicians at some point needs to include customer interaction skills. A+, by testing those, helps get technicians off to the right start in this area, too.

"Everyone's career is ultimately his or her own responsibility. Take the initiative to manage your own. Decide where you want to be with your skills, then give yourself the specific training you need to get there."

Real world skills and your A+ certification

Ben Eckart

Instructor in Computer Repair, Manhattan Area Technical Center, Manhattan, Kansas

"I try to give my students what they need to succeed—and not just as an entry-level technician. I believe that we are actually giving students much of what they need to be successful senior technicians right out of school. A+ certification, which I recommend to all my students, plays an important role in this.

"Senior-level technicians differ from entry-level technicians because of their greater breadth of knowledge. Entry-level technicians are sometimes called 'board swappers' because they are basically repairing or replacing individual components and do not understand the more fundamental issues that are often involved with computer problems.

"Anyone can learn to be a board swapper in a couple months and go to work for $5–$8 per hour, typically working in a retail store to upgrade and swap parts or to do repairs. When board swappers meet a problem, they often can't determine its cause, because they don't really know how a computer works. Most technical schools produce this kind of technician.

"But most repair shops have no use for board swappers. What they need is really the senior-level technician: someone with component-level troubleshooting skills, an in-depth knowledge of the operating system, and an understanding of electronics.

"Without that kind of knowledge, your work is often not cost-effective. You might replace an entire board, when a 10-cent piece was the cause of the problem, or tell the client it's time to replace a $400 monitor when it could have been repaired for $30. Without understanding electronics, you may never be able to repair a computer, not even by replacing every board in it.

"You have to be able to troubleshoot computers in the way that a senior-level technician can. The senior-level technician has more of a knowledge base than the board swapper does and, as a result, produces much better results and earns much more, starting at $12 or more per hour.

"The A+ exam shows if you have many of these kinds of senior-level abilities. It shows if you have a technical knowledge of the hardware and a technical knowledge of DOS and Windows, not just a knowledge of applications.

"To do well on the A+ test, you must also have the attitude of the senior-level tech: the attitude that if you understand fundamental principles, you can solve any computer problem, including ones you've never encountered before.

"For example, the test may ask about installing CD-ROM drives. The candidate may know about installing hard drives, but never have been taught how to install CD-ROM drives. If you're just a board swapper, you'll be stumped by this or other situations you meet for the first time on the A+ exam.

"But if you have the broader vision of a senior-level technician, you know that the concepts and procedures used when interfacing with the computer are exactly the same, no matter what kind of device you're hooking up. The technician with the senior-level perspective could answer that question whether it was about hooking up a mouse, a keyboard, a CD-ROM drive, or a sound card. The same considerations are involved in every installation. You'll get the answer right if you understand generic troubleshooting concepts.

"A+ tests you on general knowledge, the kind that's equally relevant in repairing PS/2s, Hyundais, notebooks, or anything else. You can deal with all those questions if you have the basic concepts, and mastering those concepts is equally important to passing the A+ exam and to making money in the real world.

"A+ certification itself is increasingly valued in the marketplace. I see it all the time in the experiences of our graduates. They're finding employers who accept the A+ certification in lieu of one year's work experience and who allow them quickly to take responsibility for hundreds of computers and for networks. Some companies even tie their pay scales directly to certification and give an automatic pay raise to those who earn A+ certification.

"Today, salary for computer technicians depends less on college education and more on certifications. It only makes sense because certification—and very importantly the A+ certification—proves you have the ability to solve real-world problems."

The core exam

CHAPTER 4

THE study guides for each of the three A+ exams (Chapters 4–6) are divided in a way that reflects the structure of the exams themselves. Both the study guide and the A+ exam have sections that reflect the major areas of responsibility for a technician.

For the core exam, those areas are configuring, installing and upgrading, diagnosing, repairing, performing preventive maintenance, and maintaining safety. For the Microsoft Windows/DOS specialty exam, as well as the Macintosh OS-based computers specialty exam, those areas are configuring, installing and upgrading, diagnosing, and repairing.

The core exam tests these major areas of responsibility with reference to a variety of technologies. These technologies are microcomputers, displays, storage media, printers, basic operating systems (DOS, Windows, Macintosh), modems, buses, and CD-ROMs.

Chapter 4 is organized principally by these technologies. Under each of the technologies, each of the duty areas is explained as it relates to that technology. We hope this organization will be effective in preparing the reader for the A+ core exam, and may also serve later as a useful quick reference when working on any of the technologies described.

Note that up to 10% of the core exam items may focus on DOS information, and up to 10% of the core exam items may focus on Macintosh information. (Also, two items on the current exam require a very basic knowledge of Windows 95.) The remaining 80% of the core exam items cover procedures and information that are not related to vendor-specific products, but instead cover fundamental knowledge needed to perform the tasks of a computer service technician.

This chapter is not intended as a comprehensive course in microcomputers, operating systems, and peripherals, but as a guide to the knowledge required for passing the A+ core exam. If upon reviewing a section of this, or the other study guide chapters, you feel a need for more information, please refer to Appendices C and D for recommended sources of further reading and training.

The specific skills and knowledge that the A+ core exam tests are listed below. Each skill or knowledge is covered in the preparatory materials that follow. We have also presented additional topics where

we felt these would be helpful. Note that for the core exam, Sylvan Prometric has identified the topic areas of Installing and Upgrading and also Preventive Maintenance as the two areas in which core test candidates have the most difficulty. Be sure to concentrate your preparation in these areas.

This chapter concludes with sample test questions (and answers) to help you prepare for the A+ core exam.

The A+ certification core exam tests your ability to do the following:

➢ Content area one: Configuring
- Describe the most common field replaceable units and identify examples of their functions and most common failures.
- Identify and explain the main parts and functions of displays, storage devices, printers, modems, CD-ROMs, and network interface cards.
- Show by example, different connectors, ports, devices, and define their basic functions.
- Describe basic testing parameters and be able to identify normal and abnormal operation.
- Explain the performance of mechanical and electrical connections among various components.
- Specify proper tools and procedures used during system setup, including visual inspections, documents, and diagnostics.
- Define the proper steps to secure a system for transport.

➢ Content area two: Installing and upgrading
- Define common drivers used by MS-DOS and Macintosh computers.
- Define the most common peripheral ports, their symbols, connectors, and describe their functions.
- Identify adjust/replace parts of a system board and define their functions.
- Identify proper jumper settings.
- Describe system logic board processor upgrading and define performance enhancements.

➢ Content area three: Diagnosing
- Identify proper, professional questioning techniques used during problem determination with a customer.

- Identify common sensory (visual, auditory, smell, etc.) indicators of a system malfunction.
- Define the basic functions of a multimeter.
- Identify possible environmental hazards to a computer system.
- Explain the sequence of steps necessary to perform logical troubleshooting.
- Define the sequence of steps to determine a faulty printer, memory problem, faulty monitor, and other faulty external peripherals.
- Determine if a personal computer system problem is caused by hardware or software.

➤ Content area four: Repairing
- Identify the correct microcomputer components required to repair a specific problem.
- Determine the proper conditions and procedures necessary to replace suspected swap out components and repair the problem.
- Identify the logical steps in a microcomputer repair process for both hardware and software problems.
- Define and describe proper safety procedures related to electricity, microcomputer systems, personnel, ESD, and parts (FRUs).
- Define appropriate use of electrical safety, system safety, ESD, and use of manual when handling FRUs.
- State the major function of each of the following field replaceable system modules: system logic boards, power supplies and associated fans, memory assemblies, video controllers, mass storage devices (including floppy drives, hard drives, optical drives, tape drives, etc.), displays, co-processors, system ROM, I/O controllers, and communications controller/devices.

➤ Content area five: Performing preventive maintenance
- Identify common preventive maintenance procedures/routines for microcomputer systems (i.e., vacuuming, cleaning display screens, keyboards, covers).
- Describe common preventive maintenance routines for dot matrix and laser printers.

➤ Content area six: Maintaining safety
  • Identify potential risks to equipment when failing to use ESD procedures.
  • Identify basic ESD protection procedures, tools, and technology.
  • Identify potential hazards when working with displays, printers, and other equipment.
  • Describe disposal procedures for batteries, cathode ray tubes (CRTs) etc. that are in compliance with environmental guidelines.
  • Describe proper steps to safely discharge a CRT.

Microcomputers

Configuring microcomputers

In the early 1980s, a number of new architectures emerged, including the ones shown in Fig. 4-1.

Each system has its supported microprocessor families, communication bus structures, and software operating environments. See Table 4-1 for a list of the various microprocessors used in today's microcomputers.

IBM and compatible systems are available in a variety of expansion slot designs further divided into two families: those based on Industry Standard Architecture (ISA), including Extended Industry Standard Architecture (EISA); and those based on Micro Channel Architecture (MCA).

ISA expansion slots are illustrated in Fig. 4-2.

Each bus design has a primary connector and one or more extension connectors for additional capabilities. MCA also adds a video extension connector exclusively for video on one of the slots. Neither MCA nor EISA requires the use of any switches or jumpers for configuring. Most configuration is accomplished through the use of software, for example, the EISA configuration utility, which allows you to configure serial or parallel ports, enable or disable the mouse, or define the LAN module video settings, memory, boot device, system board speed, and type of hard drive or floppy drive system.

Figure 4-1

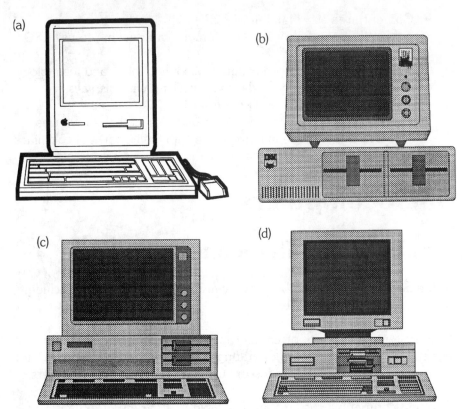

New architectures emerging in the early 80s, including the (a) Apple Macintosh, (b) IBM PC/XT, (c) IBM AT, and (d) IBM Compatibles.

Regardless of type, all communication buses have the same purpose: Distributing important signals. These signals can be grouped into the following categories:

> Address

> Data

> Control

> Power & Ground

> Clock and/or Timing

The Apple systems may use one of three basic bus structures for all their communications and expansion capabilities: Apple Desktop Bus, NuBus, and Processor Direct Slots.

Microprocessor specifications

Table 4-1

Processor	Register size	Data bus	Address bus	Maximum memory	Internal math co-processor
(DOS/WINDOWS)					
8088	16-bit	8-bit	20-bit	1 MB	No
80286	16-bit	16-bit	24-bit	16 MB	No
80386SX	32-bit	16-bit	24-bit	16 MB	No
80386DX	32-bit	32-bit	32-bit	4 GB	No
80486SX	32-bit	32-bit	32-bit	4 GB	No
80486DX	32-bit	32-bit	32-bit	4 GB	Yes
Pentium	64-bit	64-bit	32-bit	4 GB	Yes
(Macintosh)					
68020	16-bit	16-bit	24-bit	16 MB	No
68030	32-bit	32-bit	32-bit	4 GB	No
68040	32-bit	32-bit	32-bit	4 GB	Yes
Power PC	64-bit	64-bit	32-bit	4 GB	Yes

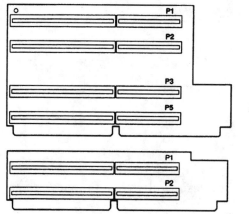

Figure 4-2

ISA expansion slots.

Apple systems incorporate the Apple Desktop Bus (ADB) to connect the mouse and keyboard devices and other serial devices. ADB is an asynchronous serial-type communications structure and can support up to 16 devices, however no more than three are recommended. Devices connected to this bus are interrupt-driven.

NuBus is a standard created by Texas Instruments and specified by an industry standard of the Institute of Electrical and Electronic Engineers called IEEE 1196. Like MCA, NuBus requires no jumpers or switches for configuring add-on boards. Depending on the model, a Mac computer may have anywhere from one to six NuBus slots.

Processor Direct Slots are simple expansion slots and were first introduced in the Mac SE. PDS taps directly into the data, address, and control lines of the Mac's processor without buffering. This is similar to local bus technology in the PC-compatible marketplace. This direct tapping enables the slot to respond more quickly than other I/O devices attached to the NuBus.

Configuring microcomputers requires a knowledge not only of the hardware but also of the software. Software codes such as those of the operating systems are, of course, essential to make the hardware perform. Software operating environments include MS-DOS, Apple ProDOS, and Macintosh System 7. Operating systems for both DOS/Windows and the Macintosh will be discussed in the Basic Operating Systems section later in this chapter.

Many modules or FRUs (Field Replaceable Units) make up the typical microcomputer. These include:

> ➤ Main boards
> ➤ Power supplies
> ➤ Hard disk drives and floppy drives
> ➤ Cabling
> ➤ Backup batteries
> ➤ Input/output ports
> ➤ Keyboard and mouse devices or other pointing devices

A computer interior is shown in Fig. 4-3.

✳ Main boards

The most important component in a PC system is the main board or motherboard, also referred to as the systems board or the planar

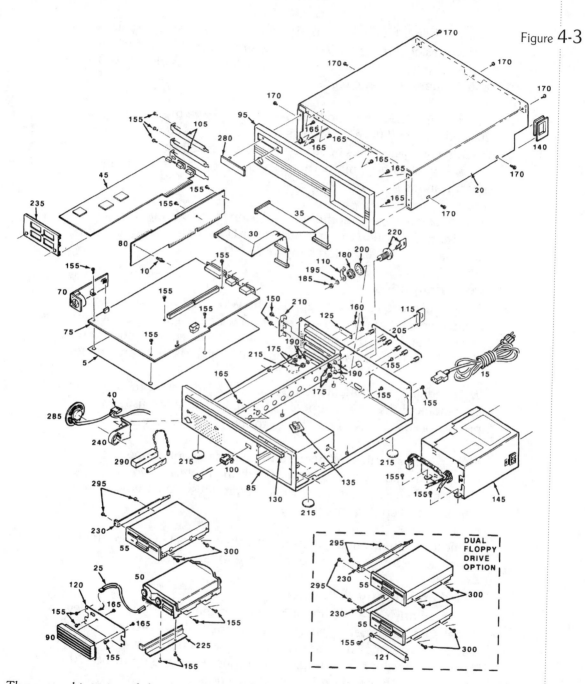

Figure 4-3

The general interior of the standard computer.

board. The motherboard contains the microprocessor, usually some memory, slots for expansion, and general support circuitry. This support circuitry will include such things as systems clocks, I/O timing, and memory refresh circuits.

Not all systems have a motherboard. Some have the major circuitry divided among different modules that plug into a common system bus board. This system bus board is usually electrically compatible with the expansion slots on a motherboard and meets one of the design specifications such as ISA, EISA, or MCA.

Most systems have a motherboard designed specifically for that system. Even though many motherboards look alike, they are not necessarily physically interchangeable.

✳ Power supplies

All systems require power supplies; however, not all power supplies are created equal. Early PCs were rated 65 watts to 150 watts. When users upgraded and added options, many had to replace the power supply also. This was necessary most frequently for IBMs and compatibles.

When adding components to a system, it is important to know the limitations of the power supply in the unit. These are usually clearly printed on the labels often affixed to the power supply.

Most power supplies today are switch-mode supplies and should never be opened unless you are familiar with their internal workings. Severe shock could occur, as these supplies typically switch a very high voltage at a very high frequency.

In most PC applications, the output voltages available from the power supply are ±5 Vdc (voltage direct current), and ±12 Vdc.

✳ Hard and floppy disk drives

The hard drive in any computer system is the primary storage device for all operating system environments, applications programs, and data. It is an important item to consider when purchasing new software, since many of today's applications require up to 15–20 megabytes (MB) of space just for installation.

Floppy drives are typically used for installing applications and backing up data, although with the large size of today's hard drives, it is usually more feasible to use a tape backup unit for saving a backup of your hard drive.

We discuss backup units further under storage media later in this chapter.

✳ Cabling

The most important factor to consider with cabling is what the cabling connects to and how it is routed through the computer system. When removing any cabling, make special note of which connectors the cabling fits into and which end of the cabling fits into the connector. Drawing a diagram may help you to remember. In some early systems, connectors were not "keyed" and could accidentally be reversed, causing the system not to work or, worse, causing physical damage.

Especially in all-in-one type systems (computer and monitor as one piece), cabling must be routed away from any high-voltage display circuits. This is because of the natural tendency of any wire to act like an antenna and pick up noise from display circuits, thus causing communication errors.

✳ Optional modules (video, memory, modem, I/O, etc.)

When reviewing any installation, know what type of connectors need to be used, where the board must be placed, the distance needed for cabling, and any software that must be installed in order to make use of all the features that module offers.

✳ Backup batteries

Backup batteries were introduced with the advent of the AT-compatible systems. These systems introduced setup menus that stored much of the configuration information required by the system. The settings were stored in a complementary metal-oxide semiconductor (CMOS) memory component that required power to maintain data integrity. Most systems used lithium batteries to accomplish this task. As long as the battery was good, the needed information was available to the system at boot-up.

The batteries in today's systems are mounted by a variety of methods. Some systems use a socket and battery similar to a standard AA type battery, while others use batteries with longer leads that are actually soldered to the main board. Note that those batteries that require soldering to be removed also require a special knowledge of soldering. Since many of today's circuit boards are thinner and multi-layered, we need to be careful about the appropriate soldering material as well as the heat used in soldering.

✷ Input/Output (I/O) ports

Proper documentation is not always available. That is why it is important for service personnel to be able to identify the various modules. Can you tell the difference between a serial I/O port and a parallel I/O port? We could easily identify a board type by examining the connector on the printed circuit board. Is it 25-pin or 9-pin, male or female? What type of components are on the card? We rely on our ability to observe. It is this skill, when properly used, that gives us greater speed and accuracy in microcomputer installation, upgrades, and troubleshooting.

Whenever you have the opportunity to perform an upgrade or installation that is new to you, take the time to look at the components involved, whether they be modules, cables, ICs (integrated circuits), etc. As new technology emerges, these modules may perform similar functions to previous ones although they may not look like their predecessors.

Serial port As shown in Fig. 4-4, the serial communication port is a D-type 9-pin male connector. It is important to note that in earlier systems this serial port would have been a D-type 25-pin male connector. Regardless of the connector configuration, all serial ports that are RS-232C operate between +12 and −12 volts and have the same timing characteristics.

Serial communication is accomplished by sequentially transmitting data over a single conductor one bit at a time. With only one conductor, crosstalk or interference induced from one wire to another is not a significant factor when transferring data. Serial communications, because of its greater voltage allowance, overcomes the distance limitations imposed by parallel communications and thus works well in

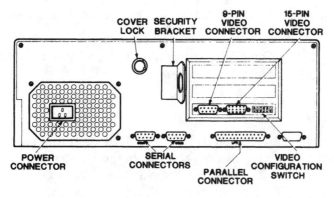

General I/O ports, serial connectors, and parallel connectors.

Figure 4-4

applications over longer distances. The maximum recommended length for serial communications is 50 feet, compared to 15 feet for parallel communications.

There are two forms of serial communications: asynchronous and synchronous. In asynchronous communications, the receiving and transmitting devices have their own clock circuits. Transmitted data is preceded by a start bit and followed by one or two stop bits, which enable the receiving device to synchronize with the transmitting device. Synchronous communications uses a single clock circuit, located in the transmitting device. This clock synchronizes the data transfer within the system by defining the beginning and end of data, making start and stop bits unnecessary. The clock also determines the speed of the transmission. Of these two forms, asynchronous is more common. While not as fast as synchronous communications, asynchronous does not require such complex interfaces.

The best known and most frequently used standard for serial communications is the RS-232C standard. This standard was developed by the EIA (Electronics Industries Association) so that devices from one manufacturer could be plugged directly into products from another manufacturer. The standard defines connector pin assignments for data signals, control signals, timing signals, and electrical grounds to ensure compatibility.

The primary signal lines typically used in a serial data transfer between a computer and a printer include:

> Serial Data Out (TxD), the output line over which data is transmitted from the computer to the printer.

> Serial Data Receive (RxD), input to the computer to accept serial data from serial device.

> Data Terminal Ready (DTR), an output from the transmitting device that informs the receiving hardware that data is ready to be transferred. This line is usually connected to the Data Set Ready (DSR) input on the receiving hardware.

> Data Set Ready (DSR), an input to the receiving hardware from the transmitting device that informs the receiving device that data is ready.

> System Ground, the ground reference voltage between the computer and the printer.

When dealing with serial communication signals, bear in mind whether you are referring to the computer side or the printer side of the connections. For example, TxD (transmit) on the computer side is connected to RxD (receive) on the printer side. So, to verify that the computer is transmitting data to the printer, the technician will monitor the receive pin on the printer. Also, make sure that both devices, transmitting and receiving, are configured identically. All details for serial communications, such as baud rate, number of stop bits, and type of parity, must be addressed before transmission. Typically this is set up through the software installation.

Parallel communications port Refer to Fig. 4-4 for a depiction of the parallel connector.

Parallel communication signals are separated into two groups: data and control. The data group consists of all signal lines that transfer data, while the control group handles all of the control functions or handshaking functions—the signals that devices send to each other to confirm readiness to transmit or to receive.

It is called parallel because of eight parallel conductors used to transfer data at one time. In early parallel communications, the port was

unidirectional; today, it is bi-directional connecting to a host of devices that are both unidirectional and bi-directional.

The primary control signals are:

➤ Acknowledge, input from parallel device that it has received data and is ready for more.

➤ AutoFeed. The CPU typically sets this line low to tell a printer to generate an automatic line feed.

➤ Busy, input from the parallel device that it is busy and cannot receive information at present time.

➤ Error. The parallel device can assert this line low to indicate an error.

➤ Grounds, electrical ground/chassis ground.

➤ Init (Initialize). The CPU uses this line to send an initialization pulse to the parallel device.

➤ Slct (Select). The parallel device sets this line high to acknowledge Slctin (see below).

➤ Slctin (Select input). The printer is selected when this line is asserted low.

➤ Strobe-Asserted, which tells the receiving device that valid information is present on the data lines.

➤ Paper End, the "paper out" indicator from the printing device.

The remaining lines of the parallel connector are the parallel data lines, PD0 to PD7.

Understanding how signals operate together enables you to examine each signal and determine if it is functioning properly. For example, the printer (a parallel device) must be initialized by the computer. This is accomplished by the INIT signal. Then the Slctin (Select Input) is used to select the printer, and the printer acknowledges this by sending a signal back called Slct (Select).

A strobe signal is used to tell the receiving device that valid information is present on the data lines and, if the BUSY signal is not

indicating that the printer is busy, transmission will take place. After the printer has received data and is ready for more, it sends an acknowledge signal back to the computer.

Installing and upgrading microcomputers

Many people are interested in doing anything that will boost the performance of their computers. They want increased clock speeds, more powerful microprocessors, and mega memory, to name a few possible upgrades.

You may need to counsel your clients about the feasibility or desirability of an upgrade. The desirability often depends on a simple question of economics. For example, after calculating what it would cost to upgrade the processor and add memory, CD and sound, the client might find it more economical to buy a completely new system. Make sure that the client is aware of all associated costs and options so that they may make the best decision for their own needs and requirements. Always let the client make the decision.

One of the most popular upgrades today is the logic board processor upgrade. Advertisements invite you to "turn your 386 into a 486," or "turn your 486 into a pentium." In some cases, depending upon your needs, a processor upgrade may give you exactly the performance boost you need for your particular applications.

Many third-party companies offer such upgrades, but all are worth some investigation before purchasing. Be wary of upgrades that cannot deliver what they seem to promise. Years ago, it was advertised that you could turn your 286 system into a 386. Many people thought they could have 32-bit power just by upgrading. What they didn't realize was that even though the upgrade board could process more information more quickly, it still needed to use the 16-bit bus that was part of the 286 system. Remember that the power you get from your upgrades is limited by the bus structure. Help your clients avoid purchasing a Ferrari capable of 150 mph when their speed limit remains 55.

Once you have decided what it is you will install or upgrade, the steps for performing successful installations and upgrades include:

> ➤ Initial examination of systems and preliminary diagnostics

> ➤ Cover disassembly and module identification

> ➤ Identification of main system components and any add-on options

> ➤ Physical installation of upgrade

> ➤ Verification of all configurations and connections

> ➤ System power-up verification

> ➤ Software installations, or ROM setup, if necessary

> ➤ Final diagnostic tests (all system areas)

Before any upgrade or installation, run system diagnostics. This will uncover any resident bugs in the system before you perform any other work. You do not want to take responsibility for a problem that was present before you got there. It is important to report to the customer any errors found—before disassembling.

Once you are assured that the system is error-free from a hardware standpoint, move on to the next step. Keep in mind that errors may occur due to previous customer configuration or configuration of the disk-based diagnostics. Also, depending on the installation and/or upgrade being performed, you may want to be sure that the customer has a current backup of all information contained on the hard drive, including the CONFIG.SYS and AUTOEXEC.BAT files, and other critical root directory information.

Finally, it is usually a good idea to inspect the environment, such as external power cords, cables, etc. This observation may provide you with some insight into how to avoid problems as you go about your work.

Before removing the machine cover, be sure you have followed proper anti-static (ESD) procedures to avoid damage to the machine. No integrated circuit(s) or field replaceable units should be handled out of their protective wrapping without following these procedures.

Many companies today have made anti-static procedures a requirement of employment, and some educate their customers on

ESD procedures. This is so that they are aware of what service personnel should be doing and can report it to the technician's company if proper steps are not taken.

The basic ESD procedures include the following:

❶ Be sure to have with you an anti-static kit, including:
  • Wrist strap and attachment cord
  • Anti-static mat
  • Anti-static bags to transport electronic circuit boards and/or components

The whole purpose of this kit is to allow you to neutralize any difference of potential between you and the equipment you are working on.

❷ Lay out the anti-static mat, and place the computer on it. Put on your wrist strap and connect it to the computer and then connect the computer to the mat.

By doing this, any charge that has built up between you and the computer will be dissipated through the connection, and you will be at equal potential with the machine.

Besides the static prevention, if you are working on a customer's desk, the anti-static mat will protect the desk from any scratches caused by moving the machine around.

After following the static prevention steps, remove the machine cover, following any instructions offered by the service documentation, if available, and identify the major assemblies installed. What expansion slots are available? Is there any cable routing to concern yourself with? Do you have to remove anything in order to perform the task at hand?

Any module added to a computer system must work without conflicting with any previously installed option. Many times this requires a good working knowledge of the I/O mapping and interrupt vectoring. Typical documentation with most upgrades will recommend an I/O or memory address, along with a recommended interrupt level setting. Also, there are a host of utility software programs that can be run to perform a system audit and show all current I/O and interrupt usage. Refer to Tables 4-2 and 4-3 for typical I/O addressing and interrupt usage.

Typical I/O addressing

Table 4-2

Device	Port address (hex range)
Serial port (COM1)	3F8-3FF
Serial port (COM2)	2F8-2FF
Floppy controller	3F0-3F7
Hard drive controller	320-32F (8-bit ISA) 1F0-1F8 (16-bit ISA)
Parallel port (LPT1)	378-37F
Parallel port (LPT2)	278-27F
Color graphics adapter	3D0-3DF
Monochrome adapter	3B0-3BF
Game control	200-20F
Game I/O	201

Interrupt usage

Table 4-3

IRQ (interrupt request)	Device
NMI (nonmaskable interrupt)	Memory parity error
0	System timer
1	Keyboard
2	Cascaded interrupts (from second PIC)
	PIC = programmable interrupt controller
3	Serial port (COM2)
4	Serial port (COM1)
5	Parallel port (LPT2)
6	Floppy controller
7	Parallel port (LPT1)
8	Real-time clock
9	Redirected as IRQ2
10	Available
11	Available
12	Mouse
13	Math co-processor
14	Hard disk controller
15	Available

Up to this point, we have exclusively discussed hardware configuration. Often we must also be prepared to update the ROM BIOS, set up menu information, and/or perform some software installation, depending on the type of upgrade.

Most upgrades are accompanied by some level of documentation. Read through everything to ensure that you are not missing any critical steps. When possible, read the documentation before arriving at the customer site.

After the installation or upgrade, run diagnostics on the system to ensure that all system components are functioning properly. This will also let you know if all assemblies were put back properly, and all associated cables have been reconnected. Many times this step is left out in haste. If possible, also have the customer perform some of their normal tasks as a further confirmation for the customer and yourself that the system is operating properly. If an error occurs after the technician has left the premises, this can annoy the customer, and it leaves a poor perception of the service performed.

Diagnosing microcomputers

In any microcomputer environment where errors are exhibited, you must be able to approach a problem and, using your knowledge and skills, arrive at a sound and expedient solution.

Diagnosing computer problems can be fun if approached with the proper state of mind. Look at the problem as a challenge or a case to be solved. Draw conclusions or inferences based on observation, facts, or hypotheses. Take what seems to be unrelated information and assemble it, like a puzzle, to form a solution. The key is observation, and remember that it takes effort to get your "clues."

All the information gathered during testing and operator interviews must be compiled to arrive at the solution or a course of action that will reveal the solution. Your determination is the key. You will find it difficult to solve the problem without a little work. Take no shortcuts.

All system problems are found in one or more of four areas:

> Hardware

> Software

> Environment (ac power, temperature/humidity, etc.)

> Input error (commonly called *operator error*)

The easiest diagnosis is usually the system that is totally dead. However, if the system does start up and exhibits an error, it is important to speak with the operator of that machine.

When diagnosing any system concern, pay attention to what the user of the system tells you. The user may have already opened the machine and attempted a repair, so verify all configurations and any other settings that can be moved, relocated, or changed by the unknowing. A conversation with the end user could provide much other valuable information. Questions that should be asked:

> *Did you notice the error immediately at power-up or after the system has booted?* Some thermal problems exhibit themselves when the circuits are cold, others when the circuitry has been powered on a while. This question could also let you know whether the system failed power-on self-tests (POSTs), or if some other possible software-related problem emerged after the system has booted.

> *Could you continue on after the error or did the system lock up?* This question helps determine if the error is recoverable or nonrecoverable. This does not mean that the error is more or less serious; it could, however, lead to the next question.

> *Did the system display an error message?* An error message can be looked upon as the computer "telling on itself." Usually it indicates whether the error occurred in memory, processing, or during an input/output (I/O) operation. Also, error messages may tell whether the error occurred in the operating environment or the application environment. See Table 4-4 for a list of common error messages.

Table 4-4   **Common error messages**

+++ ERROR: Please replace the backup battery! +++

+++ ERROR: Bad configuration information found in CMOS! +++

+++ ERROR: CPU failure! +++

+++ ERROR: ROM checksum failure! +++

+++ ERROR: Overflow! +++

+++ ERROR: RAM failure! Address: XXXX:YYYY, Bit: X, Module: XXX +++

+++ ERROR: Parity Hardware failure! Address: XXXX: YYYY, Bit: X, Module XXX +++

+++ ERROR: Parity failure! +++

+++ ERROR: Memory Parity Failure! +++

+++ ERROR: Timer Interrupt failure! +++

+++ ERROR: Base memory size error! setup: XXXK Actual: YYYK +++

+++ ERROR: Extended Memory size error! Setup: XXXXXK Actual: YYYYYK +++

+++ ERROR: Divide by zero! +++

+++ ERROR: Keyboard not responding or not connected! +++

+++ ERROR: Invalid/No keyboard code received!+++

+++ ERROR: Drive not ready! +++

+++ ERROR: Bad disk controller! +++

+++ ERROR: DMA overrun! +++

+++ ERROR: Disk not bootable! +++

+++ ERROR: Sector not found! +++

+++ ERROR: CRC error! +++

+++ ERROR: Invalid address mark detected! +++

+++ ERROR: Seek failure! +++

+++ ERROR: Invalid data read! +++

No system

Not a bootable partition

+++ Non-maskable interrupt! +++

+++ ERROR: Wild Hardware Interrupt! +++

FATAL: Internal Stack Failure, System Halted

The more we become familiar with microcomputer environments, the easier it becomes to recognize where an error message originates. An easy way to familiarize yourself is to examine any operating system user guide. It will typically list the most common error messages.

➢ *Can you duplicate the error?* Error duplication is a key area to explore because if it can be done, it may show a possible operator error.

➢ *Is the error intermittent or does it happen repetitively?* Repetitive errors are easier to track than intermittent ones. See if the error occurs during most operations or just certain ones. Even if an error is random during different operations, it may point to some common denominators.

➢ *What operation were you involved in when the error occurred, or what task were you doing?* If the operator was entering data, it could be a keyboard processing error. If the operator was attempting to print, there might be a problem with the printer or I/O port. An error while saving to file error could point to a faulty drive. Questions like these can tell you where the problem may be and if it might be environmentally caused or result from an operator input error.

When diagnosing a microcomputer, you may need to verify the power being fed into the computer as well as the output of the internal power supply. As technicians, we cannot always rely on the light-emitting diode (LED) indicators, which may also be faulty.

Here an instrument may be of help. The most common instrument for measuring voltage is the DVM, or digital voltmeter. The voltmeter is also called a multimeter, since it measures not only voltage but also current and resistance.

Voltage is defined as a difference of potential. So when you measure voltage, it is always in reference to some point. That is why the multimeters have two leads, or probes. One is typically the color black for ground, or common. And the other is red for the hot, or positive, side.

When measuring an unknown voltage, always set the scale on the multimeter to the highest setting. You do not want to damage a meter if the voltage you are measuring is higher than the setting on the meter.

Place the black lead, or probe, on ground or the chassis of the machine and put the red probe on the wire or other point you are measuring. Once you see the voltage reading, you may adjust the scale setting downward to obtain a more accurate reading.

In the microcomputer system, the direct current (dc) voltages you typically see are ±5 Vdc or ±12 Vdc. The +5 volts is used for most logic, and the ±12 volts is used for disk drive motors and serial communications.

When verifying power from a wall outlet, make sure the meter is set for the ac (alternating current) mode. Otherwise, you may damage the meter.

Repairing microcomputers

Once the microcomputer environment has been diagnosed, you must make a hypothesis, or an educated guess, as to what is causing the problem.

In any repair environment, it is important to be cautious as you disassemble the microcomputer. Follow ESD procedures. Also, before you start to remove any components from a system, be sure you know the placement of every module within the enclosure and the routing of any cabling. Many times modules have to be removed in order to gain access to others. This is especially true in the laptop/notebook environment (see Fig. 4-5).

You must be concerned with all fasteners and their size, internal shielding, cable routing, and external case pieces. Take no shortcuts—a misplaced fastener or shield might cause improper operation once you reassemble the unit. If necessary, keep a piece of paper with you and make notes or drawings as you disassemble so there is no guesswork when you have to reassemble.

After you replace the suspect module, power up the system and verify proper POST, system initialization, and booting of the operating environment. After the system has booted, load a disk-based diagnostic and run a complete system check to ensure that the original

Figure 4-5

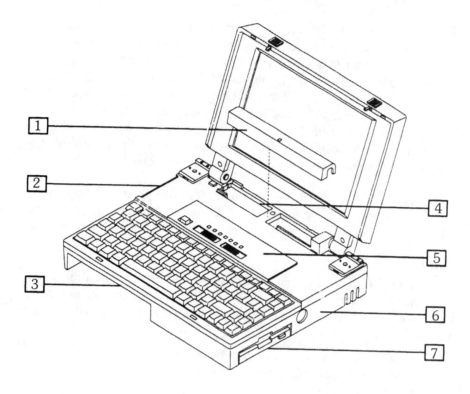

1. Memory access panel (removed)
2. PCMCIA port (inside)
3. Battery compartment
   (shown without battery)
4. Memory expansion sockets

5. Control panel assembly
6. HDD (inside)
7. FDD

A standard laptop computer.

problem has been solved and that any other modules or cables that were removed have been properly replaced. This includes all peripherals disconnected during your analysis process.

If the problem appears to be solved, then it is time to load the customer's applications and ask the customer to run the computer through its paces to uncover any latent software or configuration errors. If the problem persists, it is time to rediagnose the situation and make another educated guess.

If the customer is still experiencing errors, take a closer look at his or her software. Does the error occur in all applications, or just one? What type of error is occurring? If it involves communicating with a printer or other peripheral, it may be nothing more than an incorrect or corrupted device driver. If the error involves memory type errors or system lock-ups, it may be related to memory management and/or high memory type drivers. In the case of brand new software, it could be insufficient memory. It is important to methodically wade through all possible scenarios to uncover the source of a problem.

However, do not discount the possibility that the parts you have used for replacement could be defective. Although manufacturers have many quality procedures in place, there are times when even new parts fail.

✳ **Tools**

It is essential to have the proper tools and equipment when installing or repairing computer systems. Nothing is more embarrassing than to have to ask the customer if they have a screwdriver. Some of the basic necessities are:

➤ Simple hand tools such as a variety of:
- nut drivers (standard and metric)
- screwdrivers
- TORX drivers
- chip extractors/pullers
- needle nose pliers
- wire cutters

➤ Diagnostic software (including extra copies) and hardware such as:
- Wrap-around plugs (loopback plugs) for serial and parallel port testing
- Test and measurement devices including digital volt meter (DVM) and Logic Probe.
- A spare set of serial and parallel cables
- Gender changers
- Batteries

 # Maintaining microcomputers

Any equipment needs some maintenance for continued reliable operation. Routine maintenance for the microcomputer focuses on air

passages and cooling fans to ensure proper ventilation; floppy disk
drives with their motors and read/write heads; and some peripheral
devices, such as tape drives, used for back-up of the mass storage
devices.

Any time a system is opened, all internal components such as cables,
fastening hardware, or board installation should be inspected. Cables
could be loose, or cut from the last cover reassembly or even crimped
between some areas. Integrated circuits (see Fig. 4-6) and modules not
properly fastened have a tendency to "walk out" of their sockets or
connectors.

Figure 4-6

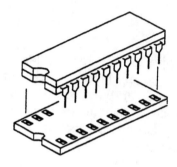

Standard integrated circuits.

Take any electronic circuit card that contains socketed components,
such as add-on memory cards, and start pressing down on the
memory devices, and you will often find one that seems to snap back
into place. We are not recommending that you remove every module
and press on its components; however, if a module is removed for any
reason, and it is in your hand, why not check it?

Preventive maintenance becomes more complicated with peripheral
equipment. See the "Displays and printers" sections later in this
chapter.

Microcomputer safety

When dealing with electronic circuitry, whether at a component level
or a module level, it is important to understand all areas of safety. If
you do not follow safe practices, you could damage the computer
system and injure yourself.

Typically, two labels are used on electronic equipment to inform service personnel and end users about the possibility of equipment damage and threat to personal safety. A Caution will typically alert you to potential equipment damage; a Warning will alert you to the danger of personal injury that could result from not following a set of directions. See Fig. 4-7 for an example.

Figure 4-7

The Caution symbol appearing on electronic equipment.

Electronic equipment offers many opportunities for accidents. Not only does it pose an ever-present danger of electric shock, but many components also get very hot and can burn you. Further, some components can actually explode if wired incorrectly or if neighboring components fail. Thus, you must protect yourself to avoid eye injury or other physical harm.

The following precautions are a foundation for safety. Following them will not prevent all accidents from occurring, but it should help reduce the likelihood to an acceptable level. You must constantly be aware of potential hazards and periodically check your actions against these safety precautions.

Do not wear jewelry such as rings, watches, and bracelets at the work place. Most of these objects are conductive and will cause a shock if they contact both you and the energized circuit. In addition, they pose the hazard of catching on components or on moving electromechanical devices.

Always be aware of possible electrical paths through your body. If you must work on energized equipment, use one hand at a time. This prevents a current from passing from one hand, through your body to the other hand. Often it is wise to rest part of your hand on the chassis while supporting a test probe. This way, if there is a shock, it will go through your hand and not your heart.

Be aware of the threat of burn. Components such as transistors and resistors may become very hot. Don't touch them with bare hands even after the power has been turned off.

Plug test equipment into the same outlet used by the computer and peripherals. Otherwise, you risk the danger of connecting to the opposite phase of the power line. This would result in a 220-volt difference in power connections. Although this is normally not a problem, there is a possibility that one outlet is out of phase with another.

Never remove circuit boards from any computer system while the power is on. Removing boards with the power on may cause serious damage to the computer system.

✳ Electrostatic discharge (ESD)

Static electricity is a stationary form of electrical charge. It is a transfer of electrons from one body to another. The magnitude of the charge depends on the size, shape, composition, and electrical properties of the substances that make up the bodies. This transfer is called electrostatic discharge (ESD).

The transfer of a static charge cannot be felt by a person if it is less than 3,500 volts. However, most electronic components are sensitive to static charge well below this level. Industry experts believe that hundreds of millions of dollars worth of damage is caused each year by static discharge. Two types of damage can result from ESD: catastrophic damage, when a component is rendered totally ineffective from a static discharge; and degradation, when a component is weakened by static discharge. Degradation is by far the bigger nuisance because it may cause premature failure of a component, sometimes days, weeks, or even months after the static discharge.

Another problem with degradation is that it can affect the operating characteristics of an electronic system. The component may pass diagnostic tests, but still cause many intermittent failures. Modules or boards that have suffered degradation end up costing more because it is too difficult to spot them in inventory, and these modules will typically pass most basic diagnostics.

Degradation is so common because of the prevalence of static electricity in the environment. To give you an example of the voltage that can be generated, a person walking across a carpet in a room with 55% relative humidity can generate up to 7,500 volts. Lower the humidity to 40% and the voltage may increase to 15,000. Keep in mind that you will not typically see a spark until the discharge reaches a 5,000-volt level.

Anyone who handles an electronic component without following ESD procedures can cause damage, and many people handle a part during the part's manufacture and shipping. By the time you the technician receive the part, it has passed through many hands. Anywhere along the line, if someone mishandled the device, ESD could have caused degradation. And if everyone else followed their procedures and you do not, problems can still result.

When we speak of ESD procedures, we refer to the material used in packing as well as to the special techniques used by the personnel of these various concerns. As a service technician, you should use a static wrist strap when dealing with the circuit boards within the electronic environment where you are working. But do not use a static strap when working on high-voltage devices, such as video displays.

The best rule of thumb when dealing with any service situation is to take your time and use common sense. Never rush!

Displays

Configuring, installing, and upgrading displays

When servicing, repairing, and upgrading monitors (see Fig. 4-8), you may find yourself dealing with many different video standards, some dating back to the early 1980s. These include:

➢ MDA (monochrome display adapter)

➢ Hercules (monochrome with text/graphics support)

➤ CGA (color graphics adapter)

➤ EGA (enhanced graphics adapter)

➤ VGA (virtual graphics adapter)

➤ SVGA (Super VGA)

Figure 4-8

A standard monitor.

The MDA standard was used in the first IBM PCs. It was a monochrome output and only supported text mode. Later, another monochrome video standard, Hercules, was developed. The Hercules standard set many of the same specifications (for signal voltage and timing characteristics) as the MDA standard; however, Hercules supported both text and graphics.

Later, as the PCs became XTs and ATs, we saw the use of the CGA, or color graphics adapter. This standard provided an RGBI (red, green, blue, intensity) digital output from the internal video board of the computer system, and could display up to 16 distinct colors. The maximum pixel (picture resolution) for CGA was 640 × 200 (horizontal × vertical).

The EGA, or enhanced graphics adapter, emerged in the mid-1980s, allowing 64-color capability. Instead of using a single intensity bit as with CGA, the EGA standard used an intensity bit for each primary color. Whereas CGA gave us an RGBI output, EGA gave us a digital RGBrgb output. It consisted of red, green, blue primary colors, and red, green, blue secondary colors. These secondary colors were the

intensity bits for each primary color. The maximum pixel resolution for EGA is 720×350 in text mode and 640×350 in graphics mode.

Up to this point, all video standards provided a digital output to drive the display device, or video monitor. The VGA, or virtual graphics adapter, was one of the first to use an analog output.

Analog output can be explained with an analogy. To represent a digital signal, all the lights in a room are either on, representing a one (1), or off, representing a zero (0). There is no in-between. So, for example, with a CGA adapter providing us with RGBI output, we view those outputs in a binary fashion. Each of the four bits may be either on or off. This gives us 16 distinct color combinations, 0000 to 1111 (0–15).

In contrast, an analog device is like lights connected to a dimmer switch. Not only can you have lights on or off, but you can have light at every incremental step in between. Having the ability to control each RGB line independently, we can obtain virtually any amount of color.

Note that a digital video monitor should not be connected to an analog output adapter or vice versa. Severe damage will result. Today, all analog adapters use a D type, 15-pin connector, while digital adapters use a D type, 9-pin connector. (See Fig. 4-9.)

Figure 4-9

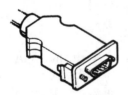

Two views of a 15-pin connector.

The VGA standard is an analog output video display, and can pull from a palette consisting of 256 different colors. Maximum pixel resolution with VGA is 720×400 in text mode and 640×480 in graphics mode.

The SVGA, or super virtual graphics adapter, standard is an analog output video display, and can pull from a color palette consisting of 16 million different colors.

In the early PC-compatible computers, all configuration was done through switches, jumpers (Fig. 4-10), or software drivers that had to

be loaded. With the advent of AT-compatible computers, most configuration was accomplished through the SETUP program (Fig. 4-11). Some manufacturers had the setup program embedded in their ROM, while others used a configuration diskette.

Figure 4-10

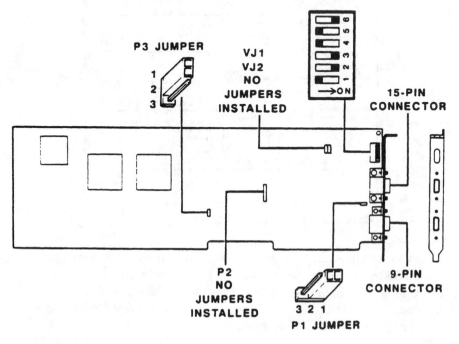

Various connectors and jumpers.

➡ Macintosh displays

Most Macintosh systems have a port (some have more than one), where a video monitor may be plugged in. Today, this port is referred to as a display port, although in the past it has been referred to as a monitor port or video port. Don't confuse the display port with another port Apple now has that supports full motion video. This port, not available on all Macs, is sometimes called an audiovisual or AV port, and might have depicted next to it a side view of a TV camera. This port is a DIN type connector.

Many Macintosh systems will allow you to upgrade the level of your color display by increasing the amount of video RAM installed. In most

Figure 4-11

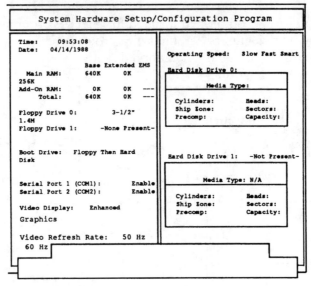

```
┌─────────────────────────────────────────────────────────────┐
│         System Hardware Setup/Configuration Program          │
├──────────────────────────────┬──────────────────────────────┤
│ Time:      09:53:08          │                              │
│ Date:   04/14/1988           │ Operating Speed:   Slow Fast Smart │
│                              │ Hard Disk Drive 0:           │
│            Base Extended EMS  │ ┌──────────────────────────┐ │
│   Main RAM:    640K    OK     │ │      Media Type:         │ │
│ 256K                         │ ├──────────────────────────┤ │
│ Add-On RAM:    OK      OK  ---│ │ Cylinders:    Heads:     │ │
│       Total:   640K    OK  ---│ │ Ship Zone:    Sectors:   │ │
│                              │ │ Precomp:      Capacity:  │ │
│ Floppy Drive 0:      3-1/2"   │ └──────────────────────────┘ │
│ 1.4M                         │                              │
│ Floppy Drive 1:   -None Present-│                            │
│                              │                              │
│                              │                              │
│ Boot Drive:  Floppy Then Hard │ Hard Disk Drive 1:  -Not Present-│
│ Disk                         │ ┌──────────────────────────┐ │
│                              │ │      Media Type: N/A     │ │
│ Serial Port 1 (COM1):  Enable│ ├──────────────────────────┤ │
│ Serial Port 2 (COM2):  Enable│ │ Cylinders:    Heads:     │ │
│                              │ │ Ship Zone:    Sectors:   │ │
│ Video Display:   Enhanced    │ │ Precomp:      Capacity:  │ │
│ Graphics                     │ └──────────────────────────┘ │
│                              │                              │
│ Video Refresh Rate:   50 Hz  │                              │
│   60 Hz                      │                              │
└──────────────────────────────┴──────────────────────────────┘
```

The hardware Setup/Configuration program.

instances where a larger display is required, an optional display card can be installed in the Mac to give you a separate port to drive a different video display. If the Mac does not have an available expansion slot for that display card, you can get a display interface box that plugs into the SCSI port.

One of the new display ports on the Macintosh systems is the High Density Display Port. It is a combination monitor, ADB (Apple desktop bus), sound, and video designed for multimedia applications and supports monitors like Apple's AudioVision 14" display. An additional adapter is required to hook any other monitor to this port.

Many of the VGA and SVGA monitors developed for the DOS/Windows platforms can run on most Macs. It is important, however, that the refresh rate that the monitors accept be compatible with the signal produced by the Macintosh. Some Macintosh systems will let you increase the refresh rate in the monitors' control panel, which is available after pressing the option button on your keyboard.

When hooking up a new color monitor, you may find that everything is still in black and white. To correct this, select the colors button in the monitor's control panel and choose how many colors to display from the box. Only colors available to you will be shown.

Please keep in mind that many monitors today in both Apple and PC environments are complying with the new Energy Star program adopted by the Clinton administration. These monitors have built-in screen saver functions that not only dim the display, but reduce their power consumption by 50 to 85 percent. To bring these monitors back to full power requires hitting a key on the keyboard or moving the mouse.

⇨ Diagnosing displays

Many video-related errors are easy to spot. Either you have a correct display with all the colors you expect, or the picture is distorted, missing, or not in color. Other display-related errors could revolve around video memory errors or I/O-addressing concerns. These more complex errors could cause your machine to lock up, or cause memory or I/O-related error messages. Usually a disk-based diagnostics can help to uncover these.

The first thing to check is the most obvious. Someone may have turned the brightness and contrast controls all the way down on the monitor. The customer may be sure he has a dead monitor. A simple readjustment will bring this "dead" video monitor back to life. (See Fig. 4-12.)

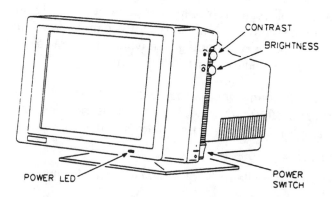

Figure 4-12

Various monitor controls, including power LED, contrast, brightness, and power switch.

The next question you need to answer with video displays and/or adapters is whether the problem is in the video adapter, the computer system, or the video monitor itself. Usually the quickest way to find the answer is to replace the video monitor with another of the same kind. If the problem is solved with the new monitor, then most likely the previous video monitor has a fault.

If the problem is in the video monitor, you must know what type of maintenance support is available for that device. Many monitors are what is known as "whole unit swap" and cannot be fixed on-site. In these cases, the monitor is exchanged with a whole working unit, and the defective one is returned to the manufacturer for repair.

Specialized knowledge is needed to go inside a video monitor to repair it. The inside is a high-voltage environment, and inexperienced repair persons can cause harm to themselves or to the equipment.

If you have never been trained in video monitor service, leave it to an experienced individual. Problems with video adapters are easily solved by replacing the adapter card itself. However, before replacing the card, verify all related configurations, because a setup error or jumper/switch setting can give you the same result.

Refer to Fig. 4-13 for a typical troubleshooting chart.

Repairing displays

Today, video displays are typically swapped out as whole units and sent back to the original manufacturer for repair. Before sending any video display back for repair, diagnose whether the problem is in the video display or the video board of the computer.

If you are in a company where repair is done to the field relaceable unit (FRU), it is important that you know the various modules you may find inside a video display. The most common modules in a video display are:

> ➤ Interface logic board
> ➤ Horizontal Oscillator/High Voltage Power Supply
> ➤ Power Supply
> ➤ CRT (Cathode Ray Tube)

Figure 4-13

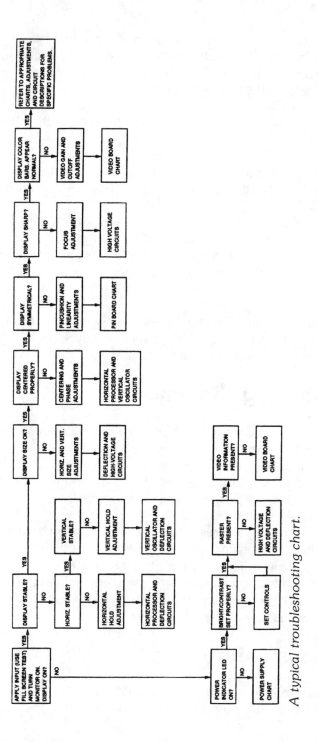

A typical troubleshooting chart.

The interface module handles the input video signal from the computer and amplifies and modifies it to drive the red, green, and blue electron guns of the CRT. This module also assists in handling the horizontal and vertical sweep signals.

The horizontal oscillator assists in developing the high voltage required by the CRT.

A power supply is required to supply all necessary circuit and reference voltage for both the digital and analog portions of the internal circuitry.

The CRT is the large display tube that actually forms the final display that is viewed. It is a glass tube sealed in a vacuum. Some of the main components of the tube include the electron guns, horizontal/vertical yokes, and anode (high-voltage) lead input.

Since the high-voltage levels in color video displays can run anywhere from 20,000 to 25,000 volts, it is extremely important to understand the proper safety measures. Always refer to any service documentation on a video display before opening the unit.

Maintaining displays

Preventive maintenance responsibilities are limited for video displays and adapters. For monitors, ensure that all air passages are clear. Many monitors are used as book ends, or book shelves. This blocks an air inlet, and could cause a temperature build-up inside the monitor, resulting in electrical failure of some components.

Whenever you clean a screen, check with the owner's manual; some monitors have a protective coating that could be damaged by certain household cleaners. The safest bet for cleaning any monitor is a soft cloth dampened with water. Do not spray any fluid at the screen, as it may run down into the monitor circuitry. Also, it is best to have the display powered down when doing this.

Displays safety

High voltage runs in the display, so the display should only be opened by service personnel experienced in working with them. For this

reason, many manufacturers do not distribute internal parts and service information for their video monitors.

Video adapters should be treated like any other electronic component that is static sensitive. Improper handling could result in immediate or premature failure of components on the adapter.

Be careful when discharging a cathode ray tube (CRT). An old CRT is like a giant capacitor. It is capable of holding a charge for an extended period of time. Even though many video monitors have what is known as a bleed-off circuit, it is always best to perform a discharge procedure on the CRT before removal and handling.

Make sure that power is removed completely from the monitor you are working with.

To perform the discharge, first locate the anode lead where it connects to the CRT. This looks like a suction cup plug at the end of a wire connected to the glass body of the CRT.

Connect a jumper wire from a ground and connect the other end of the jumper wire to the metal shaft of the screwdriver.

Take the tip of the screwdriver and pry it under the rubber cup where the anode lead connects to the CRT. Be sure that your fingers are not touching the metal part of the screwdriver, and that the screwdriver you are using has a well-insulated handle.

If there is any built-up charge, you will hear a small pop sound. Once this is complete, it is safe for you to remove the anode lead from the CRT. If you don't hear the pop, make sure that the screwdriver is touching the metal conductor of the anode lead.

Because of stricter environmental laws today, it is illegal to toss many batteries and CRTs in the garbage. Many of these items are labeled "hazardous waste" in several states. The manufacturer may have included with the new CRT and batteries a fact sheet explaining safe disposal methods for the old CRT and batteries. If not, you may either contact the manufacturer directly for suggestions on disposal or check

with a salvage company in your area, which may provide you with a safe avenue for disposing of these items.

 # Storage media

 # Configuring, installing, and upgrading storage media

The most popular storage media used in both the Mac and the PC environments today are floppy drives, hard drives, tape drives, and CD-ROM drives.

✳ Floppy drive storage media

Whatever device is replaced or added to an existing environment, it is critical that we configure it correctly. This will ensure that it interacts properly with the hardware or software environments and does not conflict with anything else in the system.

Most applications use the floppy drive to load new software, back up small applications, and load or run diagnostics. Floppy drives have evolved from the 8" disk drives of the late 1970s, to the 5.25" drives of the early 1980s, to the 3.5" drives in use today. Floppy drives, though slow compared to their hard drive counterparts, are an integral part of the system.

Data is written to both sides of the floppy diskette, with each side divided into tracks, and each track subdivided into sectors.

The early 5.25" floppy disk drives consisted of these formats:

> ➤ 5.25" DSDD (double sided-double density) either in a 320K or 360K arrangement. The 320K has eight sectors per track, and the 360K has nine sectors per track. These disks are formatted on both sides at 48 TPI (tracks per inch) using only 40 of those tracks per side.

> ➤ 5.25" DSHD (double sided-high density), which can store 1.2MB of information. This format consists of a track density of 96 TPI using 80 tracks per side. Each track is subdivided into 15 sectors per track.

The 3.5" floppy disk drives consist of the following formats:

> ➤ 3.5" DSDD, which can store 720K of information. These disks are formatted at 135 TPI, using 80 tracks per side, and nine sectors per track.

> ➤ 3.5" DSHD, which can store 1.44M of information. These disks are formatted at 135 TPI format, using 80 tracks per side, and 18 sectors per track.

In 1987, Toshiba announced a 3.5" floppy disk drive capable of storing 2.88MB of information. This drive went into production in 1989. DOS versions 5.0 and higher support this configuration.

There are four basic items to keep in mind when configuring floppy disk drives:

> ➤ Drive select

> ➤ Termination resistor

> ➤ Pin 34 - Disk change signal

> ➤ Media sensor-sensing low or high density media type

Drive select The drive select is set to give each disk drive in the system a unique address. Floppy drives usually have jumpers labeled 1 through 4 for the drive select. Keep in mind that some disk drive manufacturers label their drive selects 0 through 4. This means that drive select 1 and drive select 0 could each indicate the first drive in the system.

The hardware refers to the drives as 1 and 2, or 0 and 1, whereas the operating environment, such as MS-DOS, refers to them with an alpha character, typically A and B. Each floppy drive must have a unique address. Bear in mind that interface cables can affect addressing. For example, in the early PCs, a standard 34 conductor flat cable connected the floppy drives to the controller card. In later models, IBM added a physical twist to their 34 conductor cable to switch the drive select lines. Drives hooked to this type of cable are both addressed identically, and the drive select signal is "swapped" in the cable.

Terminating resistors Terminating resistor packs prevent random signals that are generated on the cable from going to the

disk drive. Typically, these are pull-up resistors that hold the signal lines at a +5-volt level, and the active state of the various signals is active low. This way, when a signal line is asserted, you get a clean transition from high to low.

The rule of thumb for terminating resistor packs is to place them on the drive that is the last on the cable run, coming from the controller. Most drives have an empty integrated circuit socket where this terminating pack is installed. Some manufacturers used dip switch devices for these termination resistors.

Most 3.5" drives use what is called the distributed termination technique. This is where the terminating resistors are permanently installed. The resistor value in these drives is adjusted appropriately so that the termination is distributed between both drives.

Pin 34 disk change signal This signal, emanating from Pin 34, is used to tell your system that the diskette has changed from one floppy to the next. The basic rule for the disk change signal is simple. For 360K drives only, pin 34 could be open or disconnected. For any other type of drive, disk change should be connected. In the early XTs, the Pin 34 signal was always ignored and unused.

Media sensor The media sensor setting is easy to describe. Only the 1.44MB and 2.88MB disk drives have this sensor. Always enable this sensor. It could be a jumper or a switch, so refer to the disk drive manual. This media sensor detects whether high or low density media is being used, and adjusts the recording mode, which adjusts the drive's write current level.

❊ Hard drive storage media

To most people, the hard drive is the most vital component in their system. It contains their programs and, most importantly, their data. In contrast to the floppy drives, the hard drive has greater storage capabilities, faster speeds, and is more delicate.

Because of its delicacy, it is important that data on the hard drive be backed up. Surprisingly, many users are not familiar with the term "backup" and need to be educated about its importance. End users are responsible for backing up their own systems. (Keep in mind that we are all end users when it comes to our own systems.)

From a hardware standpoint, there are four items to pay attention to in dealing with hard disk drives:

➤ Drive select

➤ Terminating resistor

➤ Interface type

➤ ROM setup (drive type) (AT type systems only)

Drive select Setting the drive select jumper for the hard drive is almost the same as setting it for floppy disk drives. If multiple drives are being used, all drives must be set for the same select, depending on the type of cable being used. (See discussion of "swaps in the cable" above.)

Terminating resistor As with floppy drives, the terminating resistor pack should always be installed in the drive that is last on the cable, or furthest from the controller. Do not discard any terminating packs since they may come in handy later.

Interface type Several types of hard disk drive interfaces can be used in the microcomputer environment:

➤ ST-506/412

➤ ESDI

➤ IDE

➤ SCSI

The ST-506/412 interface, developed by Seagate Technologies around 1980, was the popular interface in most early PCs. This interface was used for the hard drive for the Seagate ST506, which was a 5.25", full height drive, and had the capacity to store 5MB of information when formatted. Later, Seagate developed the ST-412 drive, which was also a 5.25", full height drive, but stored 10MB of information when formatted. The one thing that made this interface popular was ease of installation. Cabling and hookups were the same between the 506 and the 412, and the only changes made were to drivers located in the setup menu for drive type selection.

Enhanced small device interface (ESDI) is a specialized hard disk drive and tape drive interface developed in 1983 by Maxtor Corporation. ESDI is a high-speed interface, capable of transferring information at 24 megabits per second. (Most applications limited this to 10–15 megabits per second.) Unlike the ST506/412 interface, ESDI did not require use of a setup program for selecting drive type. The ESDI interface enables the controller or motherboard ROM BIOS to read the parameters directly from the hard drive.

The integrated drive electronics (IDE) interface incorporates the controller directly on the hard drive. You may be familiar with some of the early IDE configurations known as "hard cards." This arrangement simplified installation because there were no separate data/control cables to attach. One cable provided all of the necessary signal interface to the main system.

There are three types of IDE interfaces, based primarily on the architecture of the systems where they are used:

> ➤ XT IDE (8-bit)
> ➤ AT IDE (16-bit)
> ➤ MCA IDE (Micro-channel 16-bit)

The small computer system interface (SCSI), pronounced "scuzzy," is not a disk interface, but a systems-level interface, which allows you to plug up to eight controllers into a single SCSI system, so they can communicate with each other. One of these must be a host adapter, which functions as the main interface to the system.

When you purchase a SCSI drive, you are getting the drive, controller, and SCSI adapter in one circuit. This is usually referred to as an embedded SCSI drive. Embedded SCSI drives allow you to attach seven hard disk drives to one host adapter.

In many cases, the controller portion that communicates directly with the hard drive may be ESDI or ST 506/412. You do not know this since, as mentioned earlier, all the circuitry is built into one device. Apple Computer used a SCSI port to add expandability to their Macintosh line.

SCSI is a standard in the same way that RS-232C is a standard; however, the SCSI standard defines only hardware connections, not any driver specifications.

SCSI-2 was introduced in 1991 and added new commands and functionality. These enhancements, which include caching, command queuing and power management, increased its performance and flexibility. The SCSI-2 protocol doubled the physical speed of the SCSI bus signals to allow faster data transfers, and the Wide-SCSI specification doubled the width of the data path from eight bits to sixteen bits to allow greater amounts of data to be transferred between SCSI devices and the host computer. SCSI-3 is expected in the marketplace soon.

CD-ROM setup The fourth thing to consider when configuring hard disk drives is the CD-ROM, the compact disc read only memory. CD-ROM technology was developed by Phillips and Sony in 1983. CD-ROM discs can store approximately 600MB of information with access times up to 380 milliseconds, and data transfer rates of 1.2 megabits per second. These devices are used extensively today in many multimedia systems.

For more information on CD-ROMs, see the CD-ROM section beginning on page 148.

✳ Tape drive storage media

With the advent of larger hard drives, the floppy disk backup routine is giving way to the use of tape backup systems. Tape backup devices are available in configurations supporting hundreds of MB and more. They may not be the quickest devices; however, they can be set up to perform backups without operator intervention, which allows users to schedule backups for the night.

Tape backup devices can be classified by the type of media used, the interface used, or the software used.

Type of media

➤ DC-600 cartridges

➤ DC-2000 cartridges

- ➤ 4mm Digital audio tape (DAT)

- ➤ Datagrade 8mm tapes (Note: Do not use video grade 8mm tape—it can cause permanent head damage.)

- ➤ Digital linear tape (DLT)—a digital standard capable of storing 6GB on a linear tape, with a backup rate typically approaching 48MB per minute. High-end applications are also available in 20GB capacities.

- ➤ Emerging technologies also include the Travan media, though these are not covered in the current version of the A+ exams.

The DC-600 units can store from 60MB to 525MB or more, depending on format and the quality of tape used. DC 2000 cartridges only store 4080MB and are suitable for low-end applications. The 4mm digital audio tapes are available up to 8GBs; and 8mm cartridges typically come in two sizes: 2.2GB or 5GB. The 4mm digital audio tapes and the 8mm cartridges, because of their larger capacity, are ideal for network server applications.

Interface

- ➤ Existing floppy controller QIC-02

- ➤ Small Computer Systems Interface (SCSI)

- ➤ Stand-alone QIC-02

- ➤ Parallel port (very popular in the small business and home market)

- ➤ Integrated Drive Electronics-IDE (quickly emerging as a viable backup interface)

In early PC/XT environments, with their multiple drive floppy controllers, you could use the extra connector to hook up a tape backup device. Although economical, these were very slow, limited to about 40MB, and the tapes generally had to be formatted before use. The QIC-02 interface, available as a stand-alone interface, was designed exclusively for a tape backup environment. This interface can back up at a rate of 5MB per minute. SCSI allows faster backup rates; however, the speed is typically limited by the tape drive, the software data compression scheme, and the directory file structure.

Software A variety of software is used for backup on tape drives. Make sure that the software is capable of backing up an entire partition (a file-by-file backup). This should also include the capability to restore file-by-file. Other important features are the ability to run on a network and to be completely verified. Be sure that the software supports the drive and interface you are using. Many packages, because of their support complexities, now ship separate configurations for SCSI/IDE and floppy/parallel.

✳ CD-ROM drive storage media

CD ROMs are considered separately in their own section, beginning on page 148.

 # Diagnosing storage media

✳ Floppy drives

When diagnosing any failure of storage media, you must take into account everything involved with the operation you were performing when the error occurred. In the case of a floppy drive access, whether read or write, a number of things are involved:

> ➤ Diskettes

> ➤ Disk drive

> ➤ Interface cable

> ➤ Power cables

> ➤ Floppy controller card

> ➤ System board

> ➤ Operating environment configuration

> ➤ Software setup

> ➤ Firmware setup (code in the ROM)

Hardware failures can involve any circuitry within the disk drive itself, or the controller card that is plugged into the expansion slot of a microcomputer.

The disk drive is comprised of electronic circuitry, mechanical assemblies, and drive motors. That is why, with any diagnosis, the first step of observing is so important. Look for loose cable, broken belts on some earlier drives, or even dirty read/write heads. Often, a few minutes spent observing can save you hours of effort.

Any time you encounter a floppy drive error, the easiest test is to try another diskette. Diskettes can be corrupted, both magnetically and physically. Or, if they were written to by another device, there may be some incompatibility between the two devices. Next, check another simple thing: are the devices getting power? Check to see if all related boards and/or modules are properly seated in their connectors and that the contacts are not dirty, causing a bad connection.

If everything is connected and properly installed, including any software, and the errors occur with more than one diskette, the problem may be with the disk drive or the controller. If there is more than one floppy drive and the other drive works, it is less likely that the controller is at fault.

✳ Hard drives

In the case of a hard drive, the elements to consider include:

> Hard drive

> Interface cable

> Power cables

> Hard drive controller card if applicable

> System board

> Operating environment configuration

> Software setup

> Firmware setup (code in the ROM)

The hard disk drive is comprised of electronic circuitry, mechanical assemblies, and drive motors. Unlike the floppy drive, the hard disk drive is a sealed unit and cannot be opened outside a special "clean room." However, you can and should make sure that all cables and connections are properly made. If any connections are in doubt, remove the cable and/or connector and remake the connection.

If the hard drive fails to boot, take a bootable floppy disk and boot the system on the floppy drive. When you get to the A> prompt, try to log over to the hard drive. If that is successful, it is likely that only the "boot track" on the hard drive is bad, or corrupted. If this is not successful, the problem may lie in the hard drive itself, or possibly the ROM setup code. As always, verify any configuration settings before replacing any hardware components.

✳ Tape media

In the case of tape media, the elements to consider include:

➤ Tape cartridges or media

➤ Tape drive

➤ Interface cable

➤ Power cables

➤ Interface or controller card

➤ System board

➤ Operating system environment

➤ Software setup

➤ Firmware setup (code in the ROM)

The tape drive is comprised of electronic circuitry, mechanical assemblies, and drive motors.

Any time a tape drive error occurs, the easiest test is to try another tape cartridge. Like diskettes, tape cartridges can be corrupted, both magnetically and physically. Or, if they were written to by another device, there may be some incompatibility between the two devices.

If another tape cartridge works, then discard the previous one that caused the error.

If the tape cartridge is not the problem, carefully inspect the interface and power connections. Verify the configuration of the installed hardware. Finally, if necessary, replace any defective components.

 # Repairing storage media

Today, the hardware environment is so highly modularized that there is not much you can do for a floppy drive or a hard drive except to replace the entire unit if it is defective. The same holds true for any controllers and cabling found to be bad.

However, when replacing, pay attention to the physical installation of the drives in question. You must have the correct screws, brackets, and face plates for the specific drive and system you are working with. Many manufacturers use different brackets or slide rails depending on the design of their chassis. Because these rails are unique to a particular manufacturer, it is important that you remove them from the defective drive, and install them on the new drive in the system. Don't make the mistake of sending them back with the old drive.

 # Maintaining storage media

Floppy drives can be treated pretty much like cassette tape decks. An occasional cleaning and lubricating is a good practice. Also, the read/write heads can be cleaned using a special swab with some 99% isopropyl alcohol. Do not use rubbing alcohol because this usually contains lanolin and may coat the read/write heads.

If you are not experienced with the workings of floppy drives, find some defective units to practice with. Never use the customer's drives for your education. Many heads on floppy drives have very fine wires connected to them, and if you are not aware of their presence, you could inadvertently damage them. The best insurance before performing any type of preventive maintenance is to review any literature supplied with the drives. And if you are not sure that a lubricant is safe to use, don't use it.

For most hard drives, it is critical to keep a current backup of the system, and software utilities are needed to defragment the drive from time to time. It is also a good idea to make sure the customer has a current backup of the hard drive before performing any work.

Normal microcomputer preventive maintenance will ensure that all air vents on the computer are free of any obstructions including dust and dirt and so ensure that the hard drive is getting proper ventilation. Improper ventilation will cause the computer to run at unsafe temperatures.

Never assume that it is all right to run an enhancement utility on a customer's drive. Usually it is best to leave the software side of things to the customer, unless you are instructed otherwise.

With tape media, it is always important to keep the read/write heads clean. Dirt accumulates as the tape media are used and can cause problems with read/write operations.

It is very important to follow the manufacturer's recommended procedures and to use manufacturer-recommended cleaning kits when cleaning various tape media. Materials and procedures that are safe for one system will not necessarily be safe for another.

Storage media safety

Storage media should be handled with the same adherence to ESD practices you would use with any electronic component. If the device is to be transported, make sure that it is properly packaged and shipped. See that the hard drive heads have been parked. Older PCs use a utility called "park" or "ship," but for systems made within the last six or seven years, the drives automatically go to a safety zone when power is turned off.

Printers

Configuring, installing, and upgrading printers

Aside from their printing method, printers can be discussed in terms of their internal software control (ROM), hardware interface between devices, and mechanical operations.

✳ **Software control**

As with any computer, the microprocessor within a printer must have programs to execute. Many, if not all, operations are under software control. The instructions or programs can come from the external computer via the interface, or from a set of programs located within ROM in the printer's internal circuitry. RAM internal to the printer is used to store any externally generated instructions as well as the characters to be printed.

In addition to the data received from the computer, the printer's microprocessor receives input from a variety of sensors located within the printer. These include configuration switches, paper sensors, and toner sensors.

✳ **Hardware interface**

The hardware interface or physical connections between the printer and the computer include the I/O ports, cabling, and interface board on the printer.

 # Mechanical operations

Mechanical operations of the printer involve the mechanical assemblies that ensure proper movement of the paper as well as movement of the printhead. Paper movers include the platen motors, tractor feed assemblies, and various sensors.

The printer's main purpose is to transport paper and transfer images to the paper. It is the method of image transfer that distinguishes the main categories of printer: dot matrix, thermal, inkjet, and laser. Each image-transfer technology has its own methods of repair and maintenance. Each is discussed separately later.

When installing any new printer, set it up and test it locally before connecting it to the computer system or network. Unpack it, connect the power, load the paper, and run self-tests. If these tests are not successful, there is no use hooking it to the system and adding more variables to the problem. There are several steps to keep in mind during the initial installation and configuration of any printer. They are:

➤ Initial examination of systems (or peripherals) and preliminary tests

➤ Identification of components

➤ Physical installation

➤ Verification of configurations and connections

➤ System (or peripheral) power-up verification

➤ Software installation, or ROM setup, if necessary

➤ Final diagnostics of entire system

✳ Dot matrix printers

All dot matrix printers form characters by combining groups of dots, and they operate in one of two modes: the font mode or the dot-addressable mode.

In the font mode, the printhead's activity is controlled by a character-coded table in ROM, located within the printer's internal circuitry. The computer transmits the data, which is accepted and processed by the printer's electronic interface. Each bit of this data points to a block of matrix data within this ROM. Using this technique, a complete character can be generated from a single unit of input data. It's also possible with this method to define not only the character but the font type using a table within this ROM.

In the dot-addressable mode, a separate input is required for each printed dot within a single character. For dot matrix printers, the dot-addressable mode is more flexible than font mode because users are not limited to the font defined by ROM but can define fonts by their own dot-addressable data. The disadvantage is that dot-addressable mode operates at reduced speeds. Most printers can be operated in either dot-addressable or font mode, but most are typically used in the font mode.

The printhead on a dot matrix printer is a series of pins arranged vertically and driven by a solenoid (a resistive coil). Early dot matrix printheads had seven pins, the later models have as many as twenty-four.

As the solenoids that drive these pins on the printhead are energized, they extend out from the printhead and strike the print ribbon against

the paper, thus producing a dot where the strike occurs. The printhead traverses the paper horizontally and strikes dots as it goes. It takes several passes to form one character line. These lines are similar to the scan lines on the video display, but obviously much slower.

The color of the output produced is dependent on the color of the print ribbon installed in the printer. Early models of dot matrix printers had a single color ink ribbon; many of the later models have multiple color ribbons with the ability to produce color output.

✳ Thermal printers

Like dot matrix printers, thermal printers also have a printhead with many vertical dots; however, instead of being an electromechanical device, they are heat generating. Printheads in these devices use an electrical potential and a resistive element to produce heat on the printhead. The heat, when applied to paper of a special type, transfers characters without the need of an ink ribbon.

All dot matrix and thermal printers incorporate the use of electric motors. Typically, each printer requires two motors: one for paper transport, and one for printhead movement. Depending on the type of paper feed, the paper motor rotates either the platen or the tractor feed assembly to move paper through the printer.

✳ Inkjet printers

Unlike dot matrix and thermal printers, where contact with the paper is required, the inkjet printer is a no-impact technology. Instead, ink is "spray-painted" onto a page. Two methods can be used to accomplish this. One is continuous feed; the other, drop on demand. In a continuous feed printhead, the ink is fed to the printhead through a pressurized supply line.

An oscillating chamber breaks up the ink flow and shoots from a single nozzle one droplet at a time at very high speed. The droplets are electrically charged so that they can either be deflected out of the printhead or recycled back into a main reservoir through an ink recovery port. Deflection is accomplished in the same manner that a CRT electron beam is deflected, using deflection plates. Continuous flow is typically limited to industrial applications.

Drop on demand technology is a much simpler and more reliable printing method. Ink droplets are only produced where and when they are needed. This eliminates the need for filtering, solvents, vacuum, and pressure. These printheads are a series of fine nozzles, each about one-third the diameter of a human hair, arranged in vertical sets of 9, 12, or, 24, similar to the arrangement of pins on a dot matrix printer.

Ink reaches each nozzle through a set of open channels and is gravity-fed from a small ink reservoir. In many cases, this reservoir is built into the printhead. Ink pumps in each channel break up the ink and form individual droplets that eject onto the paper. Many of today's disposable printheads are of this type.

✳ **Laser printers**

Laser printers differ from the others in that they use a process that involves light, electricity, chemistry, pressure, and heat. This process is referred to as electrostatic. The main components used in the electrostatic process are listed here:

➢ Photosensitive drum

➢ Cleaning blade

➢ Erasure lamp

➢ Primary corona

➢ Writing mechanism

➢ Toner

➢ Transfer corona

➢ Fusing roller(s)

Referring to Fig. 4-14, note that the photosensitive drum and the cleaning blade are inside the print cartridge. The erasure lamp is a part of the printhead, and the writing mechanism is the printhead. The primary corona and the transfer corona are part of the lower frame assembly. Toner is included in the print cartridge. And the fusing roller is a part of the fuser.

Figure 4-14

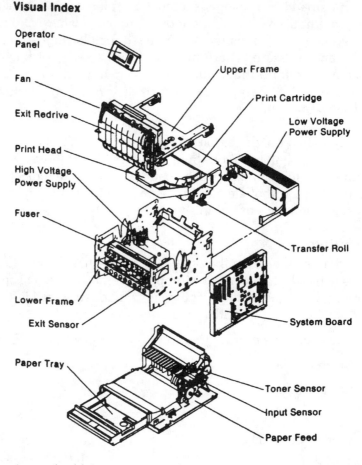

A standard laser printer.

Complete image development is a six-step process involving all of the components listed above. The six steps in the cycle are:

❶ Cleaning

❷ Charging

❸ Writing

❹ Developing

❺ Transferring

❻ Fusing

During the six steps of the cycle, the laser printer charges a photosensitive drum. (The drum is an aluminum cylinder coated with a nontoxic organic compound that conducts electricity when exposed to light.) The charge on the drum attracts toner from the toner cartridge. As paper is fed through the printer, the photosensitive drum rotates and comes in contact with the paper. Because of the unlike charges between the drum and paper, the toner transfers from the drum to the paper. Then the fuser assembly presses and heats the toner to bond it to the paper.

Now let's look at the process in more detail:

Cleaning To begin the cycle, the photosensitive drum must be cleaned and electrically erased.

Cleaning is accomplished with a rubber blade applied across the entire length of the drum to gently scrape away any residual toner. If this were not done, you would see random speckles or dots on your printed pages. It is important that the cleaning step does not cause any damage, no matter how minor, to the drum. Toner that is scraped away in this process is deposited in a debris cavity or recycled back into the main toner supply area.

Electrical erasing is accomplished by a series of erasure lamps placed in close proximity to the drum's surface. Erasure lamps leave the drum in a neutral state, so it no longer attracts toner.

A neutral drum is no longer receptive to light from the writing mechanism, or from the laser, so the drum must be charged again.

Charging This is where the primary corona comes into play. This solid wire has a large negative voltage applied to it, often more than −5,000 volts. Since it is close to the surface of the drum, and the drum and the high-voltage power supply share the same ground, an electrical field is established between the corona wire and the drum.

With low voltages, the air gap between the corona and drum would act like an insulator. However, with thousands of volts of electricity, the insulating strength of air breaks down and an electric corona is formed. The corona ionizes the air molecules surrounding the wire, and negative charges migrate to the drum's surface.

In addition to the primary corona, the laser printer has a primary grid between the wire and drum. By applying a negative voltage to the grid, charging voltage and current to the drum can be regulated. Once the drum is charged, it is now ready to receive a new image.

Writing In order to form an image on the drum surface, the negative uniform charge that has conditioned the drum must be discharged in the precise area where images are to be produced. The discharging produces an array of electrostatic charges that are not visible.

Images are written to the drum's surface as horizontal rows of electrical charges. A dot of light on the drum's surface will cause a positive charge at that point, which will correspond to a visual dot on a completed page.

Developing This pattern of charge must be developed into a visible image before it can be transferred to paper. Toner, which is extremely fine powder of plastic resin and organic compounds bonded to iron particles, is used for this purpose. Toner is attracted to the charges on the drum in the areas exposed to the laser and not to the other areas of the drum.

Transferring Once a toner image has been created on the drum, it must be transferred onto the paper. Since the toner is attracted to the drum, it must be pried away by applying an even larger charge to the paper. A transfer corona wire is used to positively charge the paper, thus attracting the toner particles. Once the toner is on the paper, it is held to the page by gravity and a very weak electrostatic attraction.

Fusing In order to permanently fix the toner to the paper, fusing must take place. This is accomplished with the use of a high-intensity quartz lamp to heat a nonstick roller. By applying heat and pressure, the toner particles are now bonded to paper.

Diagnosing printers

With the printer (or any other peripheral device), the first step in analyzing difficulties is to determine if the problem is actually in the printer or if it is in the software or the computer system. The typical

complaint heard by the service engineer is "I can't print." It is important to keep in mind all areas that could affect the ability to print. These areas include:

➢ Software

➢ Computer systems or its I/O ports

➢ Cabling and other connections

➢ Printer interface

➢ Printer control electronics (See Fig. 4-15)

➢ Printers mechanical assemblies

➢ Paper faults, for example moist paper or low-grade paper quality

One good rule of thumb when working with printers and other mechanical type peripherals is to make sure that all is clean. Printers operate in an environment that contains paper dust, ink, and oils from mechanical assemblies. These can cause paper paths to become jammed, slide rails to start resisting the movement of printheads, and other problems.

Many service shops instruct their technicians to completely clean and lubricate any printer to the manufacturer's specifications before beginning any major diagnostic analysis. In many cases, the problem is solved with cleaning. But keep in mind that if the printer was extremely dirty, the dirt may have caused a component failure.

If you cannot print at all or if the output appears to be nothing but random character generation, then software configuration is a good suspect. Often, printer drivers get corrupted, or are inadvertently changed by the operator. Within the Windows environment, it takes only a few seconds to verify the type of print driver that is installed. Accessing through the control panel into the printer section will tell you immediately.

After checking the software, it is usually a good idea to run some quick integrity tests (disk-based diagnostics) on the computer system itself. Often you could be running these tests and inspecting the cabling or the printer at the same time. It is not uncommon to find

System Board Connector Locations (Model 4029-02X)

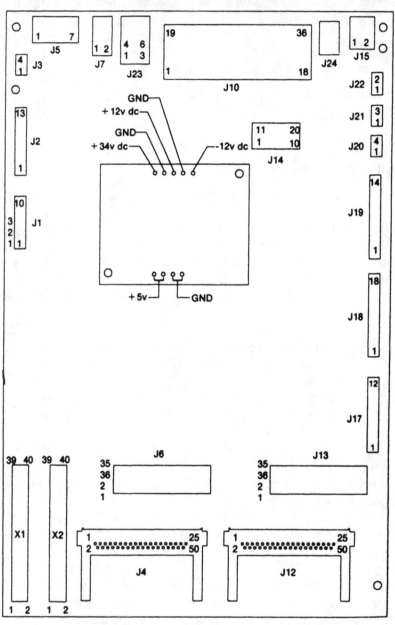

A typical layout for a laser printer board.

problems with interrupt circuits, memory circuits, or other related areas that could disrupt proper instruction and/or data flow to the printer or other peripheral.

Always inspect the cabling when diagnosing problems with external peripheral devices. You may find them stretched, crimped, or even broken.

All printers have a self-contained program in ROM called a self-test. This self-test is capable of testing all printer circuits except for the printer's interface to the computer. Usually the self-test executes some basic electronic diagnostics, such as CPU and memory tests; the self-test will attempt to print the character sets to determine if hard copy output is possible. The output portion of the self-test also allows us to observe if the mechanical assemblies are functioning as they should.

 # Repairing printers

As with the repair of any peripheral, it is important to be sure that the error is in the peripheral and not in the computer or other areas. The computer can be diagnosed with disk-based diagnostics, and the printer can be diagnosed with the self-test. Once we are certain the printer has a problem, we must look to each of the printer's major components.

These are power supply, logic boards, sensors, and mechanical assemblies. Always refer to any manufacturer documentation before proceeding with a disassembly to replace a field replaceable unit, and follow all safety guidelines.

 # Maintaining printers

Preventive maintenance for a printer is probably the most important and most neglected step to ensure trouble-free operation. Taking 5–10 minutes every couple of months could save you from expensive downtime when you least need it. When performing any type of preventive maintenance, always refer to any recommended procedures listed in user and/or service manuals.

Common steps in most preventive maintenance include vacuuming, cleaning, lubricating the interior, and also wiping down the external case. You will also want to make sure that all air passages required for proper cooling are clear. You cannot treat a dot matrix like a laser, or vice versa. Each has its own unique requirements for proper preventive maintenance. For example, years ago, some dot matrix printheads used graphite bearings which could be damaged if oil was used on them.

⇨ Printer safety

When working with printers, there are a few things to keep in mind. The first is clothing. While it is professional for a man to wear a tie, it is also a good idea to tuck it into your shirt when working on mechanical devices. Otherwise you may find your tie caught on the platen or other moving parts inside the printer.

Second, you are dealing with a high-dirt environment inside the printer, so you want to be careful with your hands around your own clothing and the customer's work area. There is nothing worse than leaving your mark wherever you go.

When working with laser printers, there are specific tools and measurement equipment provided by the manufacturers to verify that the laser is working properly. Never take any shortcuts with the recommended procedures. Also, as with any electronic components, please keep ESD procedures in mind.

⇨ Basic operating systems (DOS, Windows, Macintosh)

⇨ Configuring/installing and upgrading basic operating systems

In this section, we consider the requirements for working with DOS, Windows, and Macintosh operating systems.

✳ DOS

Today, the only ability that is usually needed when installing and setting up new software environments is the ability to read and swap disks in the drive as the machine requests you to. Not only will the installation program copy all the necessary files, it will update your AUTOEXEC.BAT and CONFIG.SYS files for you.

The only thing left for you to do is to make a backup copy of any new programs that have been added. As mentioned earlier, these files could be suspect in many problem situations. Occasionally, users may accidentally modify or delete the autoexec.bat and the config.sys files, and both are necessary for proper system operation.

The easiest way to perform any upgrade of the MS-DOS operating system is to use the automatic installation and upgrade utility that is built into DOS. This method will step you through the process and instruct when to swap floppy diskettes so that it may replace the existing files with the new version.

Whenever any installation or upgrade is performed, it is extremely important to ensure that device drivers required for proper operation of the hardware environment are installed. These device drivers may be a mouse driver, memory handler, or peripheral driver. Without these drivers, certain aspects of the computer system will not operate properly.

Each of the computer's hardware components is called a device and has characteristics that can be customized. MS-DOS uses a program called a device driver to control every device. There are device drivers for your keyboard, hard disk, floppy disk, and I/O ports. Because these device drivers are built-in, you do not have to do anything special to use them. However, certain features of these device drivers can be customized by using commands in the config.sys file. For example, you could change the language designation of the keyboard from English to French, or Spanish.

Some common drivers are:

➢ ANSI.SYS

➢ DISPLAY.SYS

> DRIVER.SYS

> EMM386.EXE

> HIMEM.SYS

> RAMDRIVE.SYS

ANSI.SYS supports American National Standards Institute (ANSI) terminal emulation.

DISPLAY.SYS supports code page switching for monitors.

DRIVER.SYS creates a logical drive that you can use to refer to a physical floppy disk drive.

EMM386.EXE simulates expanded memory and provides access to the upper memory area on a computer with an 80386 or higher processor with extended memory.

HIMEM.SYS manages the use of extended memory on a computer with an 80286 or higher processor and extended memory.

RAMDRIVE.SYS simulates a hard disk drive by creating a virtual disk drive in the system's RAM.

❈ Windows

Many PC users today operate in the Microsoft Windows environment. Windows is a graphical user interface (GUI—pronounced "gooey") that allows you to switch between multiple applications and transfer information between them.

In Windows, the computer screen is called the desktop and displays all your work in rectangular areas called Windows. Each window displays a certain application, such as word processing documents, or an electronic spreadsheet. These can be arranged on your desktop just as you arrange things on your real desk.

Windows also comes with some useful accessory programs such as an appointment calendar, calculator, and notepad, to name a few. Windows also provides on-line Help menus that give quick and concise how-to information.

Windows can run in many different hardware environments; however, the ideal environment includes:

➢ MS-DOS version 3.1 or later

➢ A personal computer with an Intel 80386 or faster microprocessor

➢ Greater than 2MB of memory (2 is usually considered absolute minimum and 4, 8, or even 16 is becoming standard)

➢ Hard disk drive greater than 100MB (many Windows applications require 8–12MB of disk space)

➢ At least one floppy drive

➢ A video monitor supported by Windows (VGA or SVGA recommended)

➢ A printer that is supported by Windows (laser recommended)

➢ A mouse supported by Windows

➢ A Hayes-compatible modem for use with the Windows communication software

When installing Windows, start at the DOS prompt by typing the word "setup" and hitting the Return key. Setup will guide you through the installation by first evaluating the existing hardware environment, then copying the essential Windows files onto the hard disk. Along the way, it will ask you to verify critical information and make changes as needed. The information requested during setup includes:

➢ The directory where you want to store Windows

➢ The type of computer you are using

➢ Type of video display

➢ Type of mouse or pointing device, if any

➢ Keyboard and language layout

➢ Type of network, if any

➢ Printer and printer port usage

➢ Application on hard disk that you want to run with Windows

After the preliminary installation, setup will start the Windows software, install the remaining files, and offer some options. Setup can be rerun later to allow you to review or change previous settings if you wish. Note that a failure to print might merely be an incorrect selection of the printing device by the end user.

When Windows first starts, the program manager application is open on your desktop. The program manager is central to Windows, and allows you to organize your other applications into groups and to start using them.

There are basic elements and skills you need to know when working in Windows. As with DOS and other operating systems, when working with Windows, a basic knowledge of its general operation is crucial. It is beyond the scope of this book to teach you Windows. Here follows a Windows basic skills checklist for the areas you need to know in the service/repair environment.

Windows basic skills checklist In order to be considered proficient in Windows, you need a working knowledge of some basic skills. This is critical in a repair scenario so that you can navigate through the operating environment. As you review the following checklist, compare it with what you already know of the Windows operating environment.

➤ Types of Windows
   • Application
   • Document

➤ Parts of a window
   • Control-menu box
   • Windows corner
   • Workspace
   • Selection cursor
   • Mouse pointer
   • Title bar
   • Window title
   • Window border
   • Menu bar
   • Scroll bars horizontal and vertical
   • Maximize and Minimum buttons

➢ Icons
  • Application icons
  • Document icons
  • Program item icons

➢ Working with menus
  • Selecting and canceling
  • Choosing menu commands
  • Using control menus

➢ Working with dialog boxes
  • Moving dialog boxes
  • Choosing options
  • Closing a dialog box

➢ Working with a window
  • Moving windows
  • Changing the size of a window
  • Closing a window

➢ Working with applications
  • Running two or more applications
  • Switching between applications
  • Arranging application windows

➢ Working with documents
  • Opening and saving documents/files
  • Switching and arranging document windows
  • Working with text
  • Using on-line help functions
  • Starting help
  • Using help
  • Finding information in help

➢ Control panel
  • Desktop options
  • Installing and configuring printers
  • Connection to network printers
  • Removing an installed printer
  • Configuring communication ports
  • Setting network options

> Config.sys file command lines
>   • HIMEM.SYS (extended memory manager)
>   • SMARTDrive (disk caching program)
>   • RAMDrive (to set up a RAM disk)
>   • EMM386.SYS (expanded memory emulator)

✳ Macintosh: Apple System 7

Though some of its terminology is different, the Apple operating environment still performs the same functions as other operating systems. It is one step up from the ROM in hierarchy and acts as a liaison between the user, the hardware, and the application environment.

Installing system updated software or new applications used to be a simple task of dragging the icons to the hard disk. Because of new requirements including the placements or replacement of files, you will find it necessary to use the installer programs.

These installer programs, which come with Apple's systems and even with the applications programs, contain scripts written by the developers that specify what files need to be placed where depending on the type of Mac system used. Although some find the installers unnecessary, it is usually best to let the installers do the major portion of the work.

You will encounter a variety of installer programs from many manufacturers, and they will not look exactly the same.

When initially setting up your printer or changing the printer that you are using, you will need to use a utility called Chooser. Chooser allows you to choose the type of printer you will be using and ensure that the proper device driver software is implemented. Chooser oversees the collection of device drivers for the various printers, and some device drivers will come with a third-party printer made for the Macintosh environment.

Printer drivers go into the extension folder of your system folder. However, you still need to choose which one you are going to use. This is where Chooser comes into play. The standard way is to select Chooser from the menu and click on the printer you want.

For proper installation of Apple System 7, a Macintosh computer with 2MB of memory and a hard disk with about 4MB free are required. By

loading your own software you will avoid loading the end user's autoexec files. You must have the System 7 on diskette, CD, or available through the network.

Keep in mind that the installer utility makes a copy of your system folder and then makes changes to the copy. At the end of the installation it "approves" the copied folder and removes the original. This is why a full 4MB of free space are required for installation.

Before installing System 7, you will need to do the following:

> Calculate available memory with MultiFinder. (Multifinder was an option with System 6, but is a standard feature under System 7.) MultiFinder runs each application in its own memory partition. Keep in mind that memory can become fragmented when you open several applications. Fragmented memory can be recovered by closing all applications and restarting them.

> Back up all current files on your hard drive.

> Update all your Apple hard disks with the new driver on the disk tools disk. You do this by using the HDSC Setup program, which updates the disk driver in order for virtual memory to work correctly.

> Run the compatibility checker to examine your set of applications and report any possible incompatibilities.

Installation from floppy disks and compact disc is the same except that with floppies you'll have to swap the floppy disks as requested. To begin the installation, open the Installer application on the install 1 disk. A standard Installer screen will come up, providing you with options that can be installed. The software will identify the model of Macintosh computer that is being used and will select the necessary files for that model.

Make sure at this point that the disk named on the Installer screen is the one that you want to install. Installer will prompt you to change disks during the installation. When the screen indicates that the installation is successful, click on Quit.

As with all desktop environments, it is important to be able to navigate your way around. System 7 looks at the world as though it

were a hierarchical set of disks, folders, and files, all available under a top-level virtual folder called the desktop. The hierarchical nature of the desktop is reflected in the way files are arranged in a list to view.

One of the first things you will notice in the list are the triangles standing upright at the left side of your folders. Clicking a triangle will turn the triangle downward at the same time that the folder displays a list of its contents. If you double-click on a file or folder, that item becomes the active window.

With System 7 it is important to have the ability to:

> ➤ View file organization on the desktop customize views

> ➤ Use the keyboard to navigate the desktop

> ➤ Use labeling to group files

> ➤ Use the find command to locate files

> ➤ Start multiple applications and switch between them

> ➤ Get help from the desktop

> ➤ Be able to remove files using the trash icon

System 7 has a feature called virtual memory, which allows users to extend their available memory by using a portion of the hard drive as a "virtual" extension to the system RAM. This allows the user to run larger applications with less RAM than would otherwise be required.

Not all Apple systems will be able to use this feature. Those that cannot include Macintosh Classic, Macintosh Portable, and Macintosh II (without the PMMU). Although these systems will run System 7, they cannot use virtual memory.

Diagnosing basic operating systems

✳ Diagnosing DOS/Windows systems

As mentioned previously, problems in the microcomputer environment occur in four areas:

> ➤ Hardware

> ➤ Software

> ➤ Environment

> ➤ Operator error

You should know how to distinguish between software and hardware errors. The quickest and most efficient way to distinguish the two is to have with you a copy of DOS, a disk-based diagnostic, and a simple application familiar to you.

Be sure to use your own software. Batch files and CONFIG.SYS files on the customer's system may be defective. In fact, it is generally a good idea to carry more than one copy of any disk-based diagnostic, since at times a copy can become corrupted. If you run into a problem with a floppy disk drive and it corrupts your disk, you should have more available.

Also, do not modify anything within the customer's operating system environment until you are sure it is the solution to the problem. It is always safer to play with configuration of your own disk.

If a port is not printing or receiving data, copies of your own software could assist in finding this out. Or if the customer cannot print, but you can with your operating environment, there is probably a software error or incorrect installation within the customer's environment.

Often, a microcomputer system will not execute its POST (power-on self-test) or system initialization. The system may not power up, it hangs up in testing, or it sits there with power applied and no other signs of life. You will need to determine if the problem is in the base unit or in one of the hardware options that has been added to the system.

Note that all modules or printed circuit boards share a common bus, whether it be ISA (Industry Standard Architecture), MCA (Micro Channel Architecture), or EISA (Extended Industry Standard Architecture). You could begin to isolate the cause of the problem by removing all option modules or field replaceable units (FRUs). These could include additional I/O ports, game controllers, or internal modems. These are not necessary to the base operating function of the microcomputer, and could prevent proper communications among the system bus lines.

If, by removing some of these modules, the system starts to function again, you know one of the option modules is the problem. If the system still doesn't power-up properly, you know that the problem lies in the base foundation of the system.

Become familiar with the error codes displayed during the power-up routine and those displayed during the running of an application. Error messages will help you diagnose the environment where the error is occurring.

During the power-up routines, all displayed error messages come from the ROM or BIOS, since this is the only set of instructions or data that is available to the microprocessor at that time. Many manufacturers use a series of numbers to indicate where system errors have occurred. It is typically (but not always) during the POST that errors will occur.

Errors can occur during initialization and reset of the various modules within the microcomputer. In many IBM-compatible systems, the error codes are categorized as follows:

System board - 100 series numbers
Keyboard - 300 series numbers
Floppy disk control - 600 series numbers
Hard disk control - 1700 series numbers
Video 400 series (MDA: monochrome display adapter)
   500 series (CGA: color graphics adapter)
   2400 series (EGA and VGA adapters)
   2500 series (Alternate EGA)
   3900 series (PGA professional graphics adapter)
   5000 series (PC convertible - LCD errors)
   7400 series (IBM PS/2 VGA adapter)
I/O - 900 series (parallel port communications)
   1100 series (serial port communications)
   104XX series (ESDI Fixed disk adapter)

Keep in mind that error messages vary from system to system. Some use the series of codes listed, while others use simple English to describe errors. This depends on the manufacturer and the author of the BIOS.

One of the most common operating errors is DISK READ ERROR; Abort, Retry, Ignore. Upon seeing this error, it is important to realize what disk drive we were attempting to read and what operations we were attempting to perform.

Were you trying to read a directory, copy a file, or load an application? The answer may help determine if, for example, there is something wrong in the disk drive or possibly a corrupt file. The most detailed diagnostic method of assessing system errors is through the use of disk-based diagnostics. To run disk-based diagnostics, the computer under test must be bootable with the following minimum hardware:

> A functioning floppy controller and at least one floppy drive

> A functioning video adapter and video display

> 1MB of system memory

All PC/XT/AT systems have a potential of at least 1MB of addressable memory, even though only 640K is allotted for user memory. Refer to Fig. 4-16 for a memory map showing memory allocation for the first 1MB of address space on a typical PC/XT/AT.

Before using any disk-based diagnostics, copy the original disk and use the copy when performing tests. This way if the disk is corrupted or damaged, you still have the master from which to make copies. Many disk-based diagnostics offer useful options such as the ability to configure a repeating routine to repeatedly test areas exhibiting intermittent failures.

High failure rate items typically include electromechanical devices, such as drives and backup units.

✳ Diagnosing Macintosh systems

Apple Macintosh, when working properly, will typically give you the "boing" sound on start-up, along with a smiling Mac icon as the system begins its initialization and boot-up process. A sad Mac that appears in place of the smiling one could be an indication of a hardware failure. Along with the sad Mac, you will also get an ominous-sounding chord.

Figure 4-16

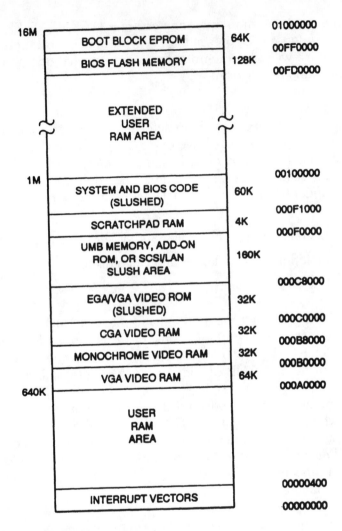

A standard memory map.

There are a few simple checks that you can perform if sad Mac appears on the screen.

First, shut down the system and verify all the external cable connections. Try to power the system up and observe if any changes have occurred. Next, insert a system floppy disk and see if that boots the system. If none of these steps have any effect, disconnect all external SCSI devices, making sure that all power is off when doing

so. If, after all this, sad Mac is still showing his face to you, it is time to open up the box.

After you have opened the system and have properly grounded yourself following ESD procedures, go through the system and ensure that all modules, cables, and SIMMS memory modules are properly seated in their connectors. If this solves the problem, inspect the inside of the machine for any dust or dirt and perform some preventive maintenance by vacuuming and cleaning the system. If this does not solve your problem, more advanced diagnostic aids are necessary.

To aid in diagnosing faulty machines, Apple provides the Apple TechStep. This is a portable, hand-held testing device that diagnoses CPU systems and peripherals through their external ports. Apple TechStep is driven by a Motorola MC68HC11 8-bit single chip microcontroller. Apple TechStep does not require the power, video, or floppy drive, mouse, or keyboard to be functioning for it to aid in troubleshooting.

The most valuable tool in diagnosing any problem is a good set of disk-based diagnostics. Many vendors, including Apple, have software utilities available to assist you in testing and verifying performance of Macintosh systems. Diagnostics are a time saver for intermittent problems since they can be set up to run continually. Let the tests run overnight, logging recoverable errors as they go.

When troubleshooting an Apple system, you will need knowledge in these areas:

> ➤ Desktop and setup

> ➤ System software

> ➤ SCSI (small computer systems interface)

> ➤ Peripheral interconnection

The gray area that first appears upon power-up is referred to as your desktop; it is also called the Macintosh finder. It is from this area that you can organize the contents of your hard drive, launch programs, and open documents. With this or any other system, it is important to know how to navigate around it.

Repairing operating systems

The word "repair" is seldom used in relation to software. Whether it be operating environments or application packages, whenever a software error occurs, it is said to have a "bug."

The process of patching or "fixing" is typically referred to as "debugging." The word "debug" goes back to the early days of computers when there were many electromechanical components, and insects would get lodged in some contacts, causing poor connections in switches. It actually became a "debugging" to clear these electromechanical connections.

Today's debugging more often involves rewriting or replacing certain areas of the operating or software environment. Programs or utilities can become corrupted or altered due to user-invoked commands or hardware failures. When this happens, determine what is corrupted and "repair" it. This may involve something as simple as modifying an AUTOEXEC.BAT file, or sometimes performing a major "reload" of the operating system, depending on what errors are occurring and what messages are being displayed.

Maintaining operating systems

The best preventive maintenance for any operating system environment is to always have a current backup. No one can predict when a failure will occur or with what intensity. If your entire system crashes, the only saving grace may be a complete backup.

Basic operating system safety

When installing or replacing hardware components, be careful that you do not cause any changes to the operating system that could adversely affect system operation. During any installations that require you to modify any of your AUTOEXEC.BAT or CONFIG.SYS files, be sure that you are aware of the changes to be made and that you are able to undo them, if necessary.

Modems

Configuring, installing, and upgrading modems

A modem is a device that converts electrical signals from a computer into an audio form transmitted over telephone lines, or vice versa. It accomplishes this by modulating or transforming digital signals from a computer into an analog form that can be carried successfully on a phone line. It also demodulates signals received from the phone line back to digital signals before passing them to the receiving computer. (Thus, the name, "modulator/demodulator" or "modem.") It must do all this in conjunction with a software communications package.

Most computers today have a modem, especially in the mobile and laptop environments.

When installing a modem, you must first select a location where the board may be connected to the system bus. Some areas to observe are the rear panel access for the telephone line, and any physical limitations by surrounding circuitry.

The typical hardware configuration consists of the selection of port address and interrupt level. Modems are configured with the serial ports (COM ports) and a particular interrupt request (IRQ) level. It is important that the modem have a unique address at which to work so as to avoid any conflict on the bus with other devices.

Diagnosing modems

When diagnosing modem problems, some easy spot checks may save you a significant amount of time. Make sure that all external cabling is properly connected. This includes the connections of the phone line, both at the computer and wall receptacle. Is the phone line active?

Beyond those basics, you will want to have a diagnostic software capable of testing the communications ports on the system. The modem is installed as a COM device (serial port), and some simple diagnostics will determine if that particular I/O port is functioning.

A number of disk-based diagnostic programs are available, including Check-It and QA-Plus. However, please realize that the diagnostics are limited to testing the particular I/O port that the modem is connected to.

If the I/O port is all right, the best test for the modem is to use whatever communications software you have, including the Terminal program available in Windows, and attempt to communicate with the modem or send a fax. Be sure you have your settings correct for baud rate, number of bits, and communications protocol.

Repairing modems

Once it has been determined that the modem is at fault, the only repair step is to remove and replace the modem. Again, pay attention to all cabling and/or other devices that are moved during the replacing of your modem.

Maintaining modems

Other than inspection of any external cabling, there is no major preventive maintenance for the modem.

Modem safety

When handling any modem circuit board, follow all required ESD handling techniques. If boards are not handled properly, they can be damaged.

Buses

Configuring, installing, and upgrading buses

As mentioned earlier in this chapter, IBM and compatible systems have a variety of slot designs in three main categories: Industry Standard Architecture (ISA), Extended Industry Standard Architecture (EISA), and Micro Channel Architecture (MCA). Each main slot has a primary connector and one or more extension connectors, which will add capability for certain systems. MCA also includes a video extension connector on one of the slots.

Usually, any configuration will require hardware settings on the option board and possibly a software installation.

Diagnosing buses

The only analysis you might want to perform on buses is to inspect and examine the connectors. You are looking for dirt or other contaminated particles that could disrupt the operation of your PC. Occasionally, you may find a bent pin in a connector.

Repairing buses

Dirt or loose metal parts can easily be removed if found on a connector. First, make sure that the power is turned off. If it is not, more damage may result when trying to remove debris from a connector. If connectors are bent or damaged, the only option may be to replace the entire main board, because in most cases, the system bus connectors are directly soldered to the main board.

 # Maintaining buses

The only preventive maintenance needed for expansion slots is to occasionally blow out any dirt or contaminants with a canister of compressed air.

 # Bus safety

Expansion slots are not a removable item or field replaceable unit, but you must follow all the proper anti-static procedures so that even if you touch an expansion slot, you will not discharge static electricity into the machine.

 # CD-ROMs

 # Configuring, installing, and upgrading CD-ROMs

CD-ROM is an acronym for compact disk read-only memory. CD-ROMs offer two important qualities: extensive storage capacity and fast data retrieval. CD-ROM disks can store approximately 600MB of information with access times up to 380 milliseconds, and data transfer rates of 1.2 megabits per second.

New data compression techniques, which can filter out massive quantities of unneeded data, have given the CD-ROM the capacity to include sound and image, as well as text storage. CDs are ideal for storing waveform and MIDI (musical instrument digital interface) sound files, pictures, and video files. Today you can even get full-length motion pictures for viewing on your computer.

The CD-ROM stores information in a digital format. To read or play back information from a CD-ROM, a low-powered laser beam reads the digital data through the reflective surface of the disk itself.

Many of today's CDs meet the Multimedia Personal Computer (MPC) requirements for:

> *Data-transfer rate.* This is the speed at which the CD-ROM drive reads information from the CD into your PC. For multimedia PCs, the MPC-required minimum transfer rate is 150K per second while using no more than 40% of the CPU's processing capacity.

> *Seek time.* Seek time is the amount of time required to locate the data on the CD. The maximum acceptable time is one (1) second. Seek times under 500 milliseconds are recommended, and times under 300 milliseconds are available.

Total time required to transfer data is the sum of the data-transfer rate and the seek time.

As with any device on a SCSI chain, the CD-ROM drive must have a unique hardware address, along with a software device driver, in order to be used in the microcomputer environment. Once properly installed in a system, the CD-ROM will take on a logical device name just like any other storage medium. For example, in systems where the hard disk drive is designated C, the CD-ROM would more than likely become D.

The CD consists of a plastic disk with data storage on one side. Data storage is accomplished with a series of microscopic pit and no-pit (level) areas. (The level areas are also referred to as "lands.") These areas represent billions of ones and zeros that form the digital code for any type of data.

When installing any CD-ROM drive, always take the time to read the documentation included with the drive. This document will familiarize you with the terminology and helpful hints for installation. There are many areas to keep in mind during installation, such as mounting hardware, cabling, and software requirements.

Typically, there are mounting rails or runners that attach to the side of the CD-ROM and slide into brackets on either side of an unused drive bay in your PC.

The required cabling consists of:

➤ *Data cable.* 50-pin ribbon cable which connects the CD-ROM and controller.

➤ *Audio cable.* This connects the output of the CD-ROM to either the controller or the sound board.

➤ *Power cable.* These connections are very similar to those of a hard disk or floppy disk drive. Use any unused drive power cable that is available in the PC.

Most CD installations require some software installation. There is a device driver required to provide the interface between the CD-ROM and the operating system. This driver will specify the drive letter of the CD so it will behave just like any other drive in your system or network. Along with this file, there is usually a .sys file provided that will interface the CD-ROM to its controller board.

Remember that most installations will also modify the AUTOEXEC.BAT and CONFIG.SYS files. Usually the AUTOEXEC.BAT is modified in the PATH statement and is modified to load any .EXE device drivers. The CONFIG.SYS is modified for FILE and BUFFER size and to load the .SYS device driver.

If everything has gone well, you should be able to put a CD disk in the drive and access it through File Manager.

Diagnosing CD-ROMs

Some CD-ROM drives and controller boards are provided with diagnostic programs. Read the information that comes with your hardware and software components to know what is available. If diagnostics are provided, run them and view the results.

Some of the common symptoms or errors are:

➤ Computer does not start

➤ Computer starts but does not recognize CD-ROM

➤ CD-ROM drive cannot read disk correctly

❊ **Computer does not start**

When a working computer stops working after an upgrade, it is typically due to a cable or connector problem. Verify all connections that had to be added or disconnected and reconnected.

❊ **Computer starts but does not recognize CD-ROM**

There are a few possible causes here. First you may need to check the installation of the software device drivers. If any are not loading, the computer will not communicate with the CD-ROM. Secondly, verify that the settings of your controller card are not conflicting with any other boards in the system. Many utility software packages contain audit programs to show you how your particular system is utilizing its resources.

❊ **CD-ROM drive cannot read disk correctly**

Verify that there is a disk in the tray and that it has the correct side facing up. Are you using a CD of the correct data format? Check cable connections. Verify the configuration settings of the controller board.

⇨ Repairing CD-ROMs

When problems occur with your CD-ROM, there are only a few things that could need replacing or reinstalling: your CD-ROM drive, controller card, cabling, or software installation. If you are replacing the drive, keep the drive rails off the defective drive.

⇨ Maintaining CD-ROMs

Occasionally blow out any dirt or dust with a canister of compressed air. Other than that, the best preventive maintenance is the method you use in caring for your CD-ROM disks. When the disks are not being used, always return them to their sleeves or containers.

⇨ CD-ROM safety

In the carry-in and on-site repair world, the CD-ROM drive is a replaceable component. It is an optical device that employs laser

technology. If you are not trained or certified in laser devices, we recommend that you do not attempt to repair any component of the drive. Instead, replace the entire module and send the old one back to the equipment manufacturer.

 # Sample test questions

What follows are sample test questions (and answers) for the A+ core exam. Each sample test question in this book comes from one of the following three sources:

> ➤ *Self Test Software.* All questions from this company have been beta-tested to ensure that success on these questions is a good predictor of success on questions in the real A+ examinations. Note that the company has more than 200 questions in addition to those appearing in this book, available in a computer-based format, and covering all three of the A+ exams. For pricing and information, contact Self Test Software at 1-800-200-6446 or 1-770-971-8940 (outside the U.S. and Canada).

> ➤ *CompTIA.* CompTIA has provided sample questions and specified that they "are of the type found on the A+ Certification tests. They are for practice only and will not appear on your test. They are similar to ones you will find there." These sample questions, contributed by CompTIA members, draw from those members' considerable service and support experience as well as their familiarity with the kinds of questions presented in the A+ exams. The questions were written and beta-tested specifically for the A+ exam(s), but, for a variety of reasons, were not used in those exams. Therefore, CompTIA stresses that doing well on the practice questions is no guarantee that candidates will do well on the exam(s).

> ➤ *The authors.* The authors have contributed sample test questions to this book. These questions draw from the authors' considerable familiarity with the kinds of questions presented by the A+ exams; however, these questions have not been beta-tested to objectively verify that those who do well on them will also do well on the real A+ exams. They are offered as an additional source of feedback about the candidate's skills, and therefore a useful tool for study and preparation.

The source (Self Test Software, CompTIA, or Authors) for each question is listed with the question.

1. What type of output device should *never* be hooked up to a manual switch box? *(Self Test Software)*
   a. Dot matrix printer.
   b. Daisy wheel printer.
   c. Inkjet printer.
   d. Laser printer.

2. How many interrupt levels are available in the typical AT-compatible system, including the NMI? *(Authors)*
   a. 32.
   b. 16.
   c. 8.
   d. 17.

3. The Extended Industry Standard Architecture (EISA) is also compatible with what? *(Authors)*
   a. MCA (Micro-Channel Architecture).
   b. S-100 Bus.
   c. Industry Standard Architecture (ISA).
   d. IEEE488.

4. Identify which statement is correct. *(CompTIA)*
   a. To dispose of dead or old batteries, just place them in the trash can.
   b. Check the battery for label information on special disposal procedures.
   c. All batteries can be recycled.
   d. Batteries pose no problem to the environment.

5. Choose two handshake signals used in a serial data transfer between a computer and printer. *(Authors)*
   a. Data Terminal Ready and Select In.
   b. Busy and Error.
   c. Data Terminal Ready and Data Set Ready.
   d. Acknowledge and Busy.

6. The term "ESD" refers to what? *(CompTIA)*
   a. Environmentally safe data.
   b. Electromagnetic surge device.
   c. Enhanced switching device.
   d. Electrostatic discharge.

7. What is the maximum length for a SCSI network? *(Authors)*
   a. 20 feet.
   b. 24 feet.
   c. 28 feet.
   d. 30 feet.

8. If, at system power-up, the only response is that the power supply fan is running, which of the following is not a likely suspect? *(Authors)*
   a. System RAM.
   b. Power supply.
   c. BIOS ROM.
   d. Video.

9. What product must be used to clean rubber rollers on a laser printer? *(Self Test Software)*
   a. Denatured alcohol.
   b. Silicone spray.
   c. Soap and water.
   d. Glass cleaner.

10. If, upon power-up, the video display indicates a 300 series error code, which of the following would be the most likely suspect? *(Authors)*
    a. Main board.
    b. Video.
    c. Keyboard.
    d. Floppy controller.

11. A CAUTION will typically alert you to what? *(Authors)*
    a. Possible damage to equipment.
    b. Possible harm to you.
    c. Possible damage to software environment.
    d. None of the above.

12. What is the best device for transporting circuit boards? *(Self Test Software)*
    a. Vinyl container/bag.
    b. Plastic foam container/bag.
    c. Shielded container/bag.
    d. Static shield container/bag.

13. Carpeting can be one of the most static-prone surfaces in the office environment. Which type of mat will greatly reduce static problems? *(Self Test Software)*
    a. Rubber.
    b. Nylon.
    c. Plastic.
    d. Vinyl.

14. What is the first step when installing a new DOS upgrade? *(Self Test Software)*
    a. Delete the COMMAND.COM file.
    b. Back up the existing operating system and data.
    c. Reformat the currently formatted hard drive.
    d. Copy the previous version of the operating system to a subdirectory call OLD_DOS.

15. In inkjet technology, the droplets of ink are deflected towards the paper by what? *(Authors)*
    a. A multi-directional nozzle.
    b. Electrically charged plates.
    c. High pressure.
    d. Gravity.

16. If a microcomputer system prints under your spreadsheet application, but not under your word processing application, there is a good chance that the problem lies in what? *(Authors)*
    a. Your operating system environment.
    b. The Windows environment.
    c. An incorrect printer driver selected for the word processor.
    d. Your print spooler.

17. The primary corona's main purpose is to what? *(Authors)*
    a. Clean the photosensitive drum.
    b. Charge the toner particles.
    c. Erase the photosensitive drum.
    d. Charge the photosensitive drum.

18. The device that regulates voltage and current to the photosensitive drum is the what? *(Authors)*
    a. Transfer corona.
    b. Primary grid.
    c. Cleaning blade.
    d. Laser.

19. Networks allow the sharing of what things? Choose all that apply. *(Authors)*
    a. Computer systems.
    b. Printers.
    c. Software.
    d. Disk drives.

20. Which of the following are important to reducing the chances of ESD? Choose all that apply. *(Authors)*
    a. Personnel training.
    b. Materials used in packing.
    c. Discharging from yourself prior to handling a device.
    d. Static workstations.

21. The 80386SX CPU supports a _____ bit external data bus and 24 bits of addressing. *(Authors)*
    a. 8.
    b. 12.
    c. 24.
    d. 16.

22. Which component enables independent communication between the processor and the external printing device? *(Self Test Software)*
    a. I/O controller.
    b. Expanded memory.
    c. Video controller.
    d. Hard drive controller.

23. In the PC/AT-compatible environment, the BIOS program is located where? *(Authors)*
    a. Just above the 0000 address.
    b. Just below the 640K address.
    c. Just below the 1M address.
    d. Just above the 1M address.

24. A computer virus is what? *(Authors)*
    a. A hardware flaw that induces problems into other devices.
    b. A program designed to corrupt data or cause damage.
    c. Not transmitted in network environments.
    d. A series of programs in ROM designed to slow down a network.

25. One of your best resources for tracking down a nonthermal intermittent error is what? *(Authors)*
    a. A logic probe.
    b. Disk-based diagnostics.
    c. A can of circuit cooler.
    d. A set of benchmark utilities.

26. Network problems can be caused by which of the following? Choose all that apply. *(Authors)*
    a. Server.
    b. Workstation.
    c. Software.
    d. Operator.

27. Transferring an entire data word over several conductors at one time is called _____ communications. *(Authors)*
    a. Serial.
    b. IEE488.
    c. Parallel.
    d. Network.

28. The inductive and/or capacitive coupling of a signal from one conductor to another is called what? *(Authors)*
    a. Crosstalk.
    b. Reactance.
    c. FSK (Frequency Shift Keying).
    d. None of the above.

29. The two main advantages of parallel communications are what? *(Authors)*
    a. Cost and efficiency.
    b. Speed and simplicity.
    c. Distance and simplicity.
    d. Cost and speed.

30. The device driver used to set up a RAM drive using the DOS CONFIG.SYS file is called what? Choose all that apply. *(Self Test Software)*
    a. VDISK.SYS
    b. MAKEDRV.SYS
    c. RAMDRIVE.SYS
    d. RAMDRIVE.EXE

31. Which of the following video monitors could accept either an EGA or CGA input? *(Authors)*
    a. IBM 8512.
    b. NEC Multi-Sync.
    c. Zenith Data Systems ZCM-1492.
    d. IBM PS/2 8514.

32. If a printer self-test passes, and the user still cannot print, possible suspects include what? Choose all that apply. *(Authors)*
    a. Computer interface.
    b. Software configuration.
    c. Printer interface.
    d. Printer off-line.

33. The natural hierarchy of software is what? *(Authors)*
    a. Operating System, ROM, Application.
    b. ROM, Operating System, Application.
    c. Application, Operating System, RAM.
    d. Operating System, Application, ROM.

34. At power-up the first code that the microprocessor has access to is available from what? *(Authors)*
    a. Disk.
    b. RAM.
    c. ROM.
    d. None of the above.

35. To limit the chance of ac line noise, you should do what? *(CompTIA)*
    a. Use extension cords.
    b. Install the computer system on its own power circuit.
    c. Install the computer system on a circuit with other high wattage units.
    d. Avoid using a ground connection.

36. The file which is the primary MS-DOS user interface is what? *(Authors)*
    a. DIR
    b. COMMAND.COM
    c. AUTOEXEC.BAT
    d. IO.SYS

37. Which of the following is not a resident command? *(Authors)*
    a. DIR
    b. COPY

c. REN

d. EDIT

38. Which of the following are examples of nonimpact printers?
    Choose all that apply. *(Authors)*
    a. Thermal.
    b. Daisy wheel.
    c. Laser.
    d. Electrostatic.

39. Dynamic RAM (random access memory) must be _____ every 2
    milliseconds. *(Authors)*
    a. Refreshed.
    b. Written to.
    c. Read.
    d. Reloaded.

40. Which of the following is not a transient command? *(Authors)*
    a. FORMAT
    b. EDIT
    c. COPY
    d. SHELL

41. In a laser printer, the photosensitive drum is typically connected
    to what electrical potential? *(Authors)*
    a. Positive.
    b. Power supply ground.
    c. Neutral.
    d. ac reference.

42. Which of the following best describes the six-step process
    involved with electrostatic printing? *(Authors)*
    a. Paper feed, charging, writing, developing, erasing, transferring.
    b. Cleaning, charging, writing, erasing, developing, fusing.
    c. Cleaning, charging, writing, developing, transferring, fusing.
    d. Charging, writing, developing, transferring, erasing, fusing.

43. Which of the following best describes the single beep heard after
    power on? *(Self Test Software)*
    a. Has no meaning.
    b. Indicates that the system has powered on.
    c. Indicates a successful completion of POST.
    d. Multimedia support has been enabled.

44. CMOS or PRAM stores which of the following information?
    (CompTIA)
    a. Date and time.
    b. CPU and memory size characteristics.
    c. Floppy and hard disk types.
    d. All of the above.

⇨ Answers to sample questions

1. D	12. D	23. C	34. C
2. D	13. A	24. B	35. B
3. C	14. B	25. B	36. B
4. B	15. B	26. A,B,C,D	37. D
5. C	16. C	27. C	38. A,C,D
6. D	17. D	28. A	39. A
7. A	18. B	29. B	40. C
8. B	19. A,B,C,D	30. A,C	41. B
9. A	20. A,B,C,D	31. B	42. C
10. C	21. D	32. A,B,C,D	43. C
11. A	22. A	33. B	44. D

The Microsoft
Windows/DOS exam

CHAPTER 5

THE specific skills and knowledge that the Microsoft Windows/DOS specialty exam tests are listed below. Each skill or knowledge is then covered in the preparatory materials that follow. We have also presented additional topics where we felt these would be helpful. If upon reviewing a section of this or the other study guide chapters, you feel a need for more information, please refer to Appendices C and D for recommended sources of further reading and training.

The questions in the Windows/DOS specialty exam cover a candidate's knowledge of Windows Version 3.1, DOS Version 6.x, and basic knowledge of Windows 95.

Note that for this specialty exam, Sylvan Prometric has identified installing and upgrading, and repair as the two areas in which test candidates have the most difficulty. Be sure to concentrate your preparation in these areas.

Sample test questions (and answers) appear at the end of the chapter to help you prepare for the Microsoft Windows/DOS specialty exam.

The Microsoft Windows/DOS specialty exam tests your ability to do the following:

➢ Content Area 1: Configuring
- Identify hardware components of the system and necessary setup procedures.
- Determine the appropriate commands and parameters to initialize media and backup data.
- Identify major system files of DOS and Windows and how they are used.
- Identify software configuration tools and commands in Windows and DOS.
- Identify methods of system optimization.

➢ Content Area 2: Installing and Upgrading
- Identify system upgrade potential and compatibility of installable components.
- Identify commonly used drivers and their functions and configuration.
- Identify methods related to upgrading Windows and DOS.

➤ Content Area 3: Diagnosis
- Identify and understand system boot sequences.
- Identify common questions that should be asked when determining a customer's hardware and software problems.
- Identify common hardware and software failures.

➤ Content Area 4: Repair
- Understand methods for replacing hardware components (FRUs).
- Understand methods for solving software problems.

Preparing for the exam

In today's IBM-compatible marketplace, there are three major operating environments that service technicians may face during any service call: MS-DOS version 6.0 or higher, Windows version 3.1, and Windows 95. This chapter examines all three of these operating environments.

When servicing computer systems, you need to understand the workings of the operating system(s) that the microcomputer is running. At the same time, you need to understand memory-resident software, and the problems it can cause if not managed properly. Finally, you need to be able to distinguish between hardware- and software-related errors.

Before even beginning to examine the Windows/DOS environment, let's look at the different levels of software code and the order in which they are loaded by the microcomputer at time of power-up. That order is:

➤ Read-only memory, including basic input/output system (ROM BIOS)

➤ Disk operating system (DOS)

➤ Windows Environment

➤ Application software: word processing, databases, spreadsheets, etc.

Each of the four areas must be loaded and must perform its specific function before the next in order to complete the total computer environment. Note: because Windows 95 is an operating system, there would be no need for MS-DOS to be loaded.

Note, too, that the various levels of software constantly interact during normal machine operations. For example, when a key on the keyboard is pressed, an interrupt is generated. In order to handle this interrupt, the processor must be directed towards an interrupt routine, usually located in ROM, which tells it how to process the key that has been pressed.

When power is first applied to the machine, many hardware functions activate. Clocks start running, system resets occur, and typically the microprocessor will access a default address. This default address is the address that the microprocessor always goes to at power-up and is usually located at the high end of the first one megabyte (MB) boundary of random access memory (RAM), which is reserved for ROM. It is by design that the microprocessor always fires up to the same address. Doing this guarantees that it accesses the proper code every time. In the order of hierarchy, ROM is the first level of software or code for the PC to execute. Without ROM, the machine would do nothing but draw power and get warm.

In the early stages of power-up, during the execution of ROM code, the machine is initialized, power-on self-tests (POSTs) are run, and the process of "booting" begins. At the time of booting, the DOS environment is loaded into memory to begin execution.

Once the system environment is established, the POSTs are run to ensure that there is enough system integrity to boot the operating system software. These tests check the central processing unit (CPU), ROM, RAM, interrupt, disk, and other circuits necessary to basic system operation.

Note that the POST diagnostics only test the basic circuits of a computer system. If more detailed testing is required, a set of disk-based diagnostics can be used for diagnosing more serious problems.

Once all POSTs are complete, the system is prepared to access the primary boot device, which is typically the system hard disk drive, and the loading of the operating system can occur. The portion of the ROM that contains the code for booting the system is referred to as the bootstrap loader.

We have outlined the basics of the power-on routines that most microcomputer systems go through in order to boot the operating systems. After the boot process, the system is capable of loading the Windows environment, and then the applications programs.

Remember that Windows 95 is its own operating environment, so you will not find a collection of files that you can look at and identify as the MS-DOS files. Some of the features of Windows 95 have appeared in other Microsoft products, such as Windows NT and Windows for Workgroups. Windows 95 includes the old features and adds new features to provide a full 32-bit protected mode environment for all Windows applications.

If you are used to working in the previous Windows environments, you will see a dramatic change in the on-screen appearance of the operating system under Windows 95. In addition to changes in screen appearance, other significant changes are:

- ➤ Device-independent color (Many devices might have their own device-specific BIOS, but they all conform to plug-and-play rules.)

- ➤ Disk and file system support, including format and file utilities

- ➤ Plug-and-play configuration (discussed on page 177)

- ➤ Network support for more networks and greater capability

- ➤ Mobile computing support for laptop and wireless communication devices

The goal of Windows 95 was to make computing easy. This has required hardware manufacturers and software developers to agree on standards so that their products present a similar interface to the user when the user accesses them using Windows 95.

 # Configuring

Hardware components and setup procedures

A typical hardware environment today consists of the following:

> ➤ 486 or Pentium microprocessor (50 MHz or greater)

> ➤ Eight megabytes or more of RAM

> ➤ Large capacity hard drive (850MB or more)

> ➤ Fax modems (typically 14.4K baud)

> ➤ SVGA video board and monitor

> ➤ CD ROM

> ➤ Sound card with speakers

> ➤ 3.5" floppy disk drive

Unlike the systems of a few years ago, many of today's PCs come with all the operating environment software already loaded on the hard drive. This usually includes DOS, Windows, and many applications. Today, customers take their computers out of the box, turn on the power, and start putting them to use.

Many vendors either include copies of the software programs on compact disks, or else provide automatically invoked backup procedures to allow the user to make an initial backup of all pre-loaded software on the system.

Many of the hardware components listed above are needed because of the requirements placed on the system hardware by the operating and applications software environments. Larger amounts of hard disk space are also increasingly needed to run applications packages, many of which require anywhere from fifteen to twenty MB just for the initial installation.

Today the only abilities that are typically needed when installing and setting up new software environments are the abilities to read and swap disks in the drive as the machine requests you to. Not only will the installation program copy all the necessary files, it will update your AUTOEXEC.BAT and CONFIG.SYS files for you. The only thing left for the user to do is to make a backup copy of any new programs that have been added. It is helpful for you, the technician, to have backup copies of AUTOEXEC.BAT and CONFIG.SYS files since users may accidentally modify or delete them.

(For hardware components of systems running Windows, as well as necessary set-up procedures for Windows, see page 173.)

Initializing media and backing up data

In order for a hard drive to accept information, the hard drive must be partitioned. This is accomplished through a transient command file usually called FDISK. This file is executed by typing FDISK at the DOS prompt and pressing the ENTER key on the keyboard. Note that some manufacturers may have different names for this file. One manufacturer used to call their partitioning file PREP.

Hard drives also need to be defined to the ROM BIOS. This is usually done in what is referred to as the setup menu. The system needs to be aware of the size of the hard drive in total tracks (cylinders), the number of read/write heads, and whether or not "pre-compensation" and reduced write current are being used.

Pre-compensation is an analysis by the drive controller of the stream of data bits that is to be written to the hard drive. By altering the timing by which data bits are written to the hard drive, pre-compensation guarantees that magnetic interference between data bits does not cause any read errors.

Reduced write current is the drive logic that reduces the amount of electrical current to the write heads as the heads move to the inside tracks. Because the data bits are more closely spaced around the inside tracks, the electrical current must be reduced as the head moves into that area in order to avoid interference between data bits.

When you purchase a hard drive, the documentation generally specifies the type of drive it is. This drive type number (usually in two

digits), when entered into the setup menu, defines all the necessary parameters of the drive to the system.

In the original IBM ATs and compatibles, many of these drive types were pre-defined in the ROM BIOS. For drives whose types are not listed, the ROM usually offers a user-defined choice. When that choice is selected, you can manually enter all the various parameters of the drive, including number of heads, number of tracks, etc.

To format a hard disk and copy the system files to it, a basic command such as FORMAT C:/S will suffice. This command instructs the system to format the C drive, and upon completion of that function, to transfer the necessary system files—IO.SYS, MSDOS.SYS, and COMMAND.COM—from the bootable floppy to the hard drive.

Before we discuss the IO.SYS, MSDOS.SYS, and COMMAND.COM files, let's consider file space allocation. DOS allocates space for a file on demand, on a first-come first-served basis. It does not reserve space in advance. File space is allocated one cluster at a time, as needed. These clusters are arranged so as to minimize head movement of the disk drive, whether floppy drive or hard drive.

There are many ways that DOS uses clusters. It may use first available, or next available. In first available, DOS scans the file allocation table (FAT), uses the first available cluster, and moves on from there. With the next available option, DOS begins where the last write took place and finds the first available cluster from that point.

Major system files of DOS

The IO.SYS is a hidden file on a bootable disk that interacts with the devices on the system and the ROM BIOS. A hidden file has system attributes and is not available for viewing or modifying without specialty utilities. The IO.SYS file is usually modified by the manufacturer to match itself with the vendor's particular ROM BIOS. As mentioned earlier, the ROM BIOS contains all the system's bootstrap codes (POSTs) and other software code critical to system start-up. That is why it is important to be careful when upgrading a

DOS from one vendor to another. If you are running IBM DOS, and upgrade it with another manufacturer's version, the two may not be compatible.

For a disk to be bootable, the IO.SYS must be listed as the first file in the disk directory, and occupy at least the first cluster. The attributes assigned to this file are hidden, system, and read only. This file is usually transferred to a disk during a FORMAT operation or a SYS command, thus making the disk bootable.

MSDOS.SYS, commonly referred to as the core of DOS, contains the disk handling programs. The MSDOS.SYS file must be the second entry in a root directory and has the same attributes as the IO.SYS.

The COMMAND.COM is the DOS user's interface. Commands available through this file are categorized as resident commands. Resident commands are available whenever the DOS prompt is present. Some resident commands are DIR (runs a file directory of the currently active drive), ERASE, COPY, and MD (make directory).

Transient commands are often called utilities. They are not resident in memory, and the instructions necessary to execute the command must be on disk. Most DOS commands are transient, because if all were memory resident, they would overtax system memory.

For major system files of Windows, see page 174.

 # Configuration tools and commands in DOS

After the system loads MSDOS.SYS, IO.SYS, and COMMAND.COM, it locates the CONFIG.SYS file if one is present. CONFIG.SYS is a text file that contains commands to configure your computer's hardware components so that DOS and software application programs can use them. This file must be in the root directory of the system disk.

See Fig. 5-1 for a sample of a typical CONFIG.SYS file.

Figure 5-1

```
DEVICE=C:\DOS\HIMEM.SYS
DEVICE=C\DOS\EMM386.EXE NOEMS X=D000-D8FF
DEVICEHIGH=C:\DOS\SETVER.EXE
DOS=HIGH,UMB
FILES=30
STACKS=9,256
```

CONFIG.SYS file.

Here's what each of the elements in the typical CONFIG.SYS file does:

Device is used to load an installable device driver. A device driver is a list of software instructions that instruct the computer on how to deal with a particular hardware component.

Devicehigh loads an installable device driver into the upper memory area of RAM. The DOS command specifies whether DOS will use high memory and upper memory blocks. (High memory is extended memory—typically memory above the 1MB boundary.)

Files specifies how many files can be open at a time.

Stacks specifies how much memory to reserve for processing hardware interrupts. For every system interrupt that occurs, it is necessary to access the ROM BIOS for an interrupt routine, which instructs the system how to process the interrupt.

Another file that is executed at system start-up is the AUTOEXEC.BAT file. This file contains many DOS commands that execute automatically. These could include prompt commands, path commands, and other DOS statements. See Fig. 5-2 for a typical AUTOEXEC.BAT file.

Here is what each of the elements in the typical AUTOEXEC.BAT file does:

The ECHO OFF command directs DOS not to display the commands in the AUTOEXEC.BAT file as they run. It is usually the first command in an AUTOEXEC.BAT file.

The SMARTDrive program, which is part of the later DOS versions, decreases the time your computer spends reading data from your hard disk. The program accomplishes this by reserving an area in extended

```
@ECHO OFF
C:\DOS\SMARTDRV.EXE C
PROMPT=$p$g
PATH C:\WINWORD;C:\DOS;C:\WINDOWS;C:\CARDWARE
SET TEMP=C:\DOS
SET MOUSE=C:\MOUSE
LOADHIGH C:\MOUSE\MOUSE
LOADHIGH DOSKEY
CD \WINDOWS
C:\DOS\SHARE.EXE
WIN
CD \
```

Figure 5-2

A typical AUTOEXEC.BAT file.

memory in which it stores information that it reads from the hard drive. Storing some information in extended memory increases the speed of access, since memory access is faster than hard drive access.

The prompt command (PROMPT=pg) defines the system prompt, which DOS normally displays as the current drive letter, followed by a greater than sign, such as C>. If you change the system prompt, you can include any character DOS can display, plus such items of system information as the time, date, current drive, current directory, and so on. In the command line at the start of the paragraph, the $p says to indicate the current directory of the current drive, and the $g says to end it with the greater than > sign.

A PATH statement tells DOS where to search for a command file that is not in the current directory being used. This command path becomes part of the DOS environment, so it is available to every program DOS carries out during a work session on your computer.

The SET TEMP command creates a directory named TEMP that is used to store temporary files that the system may create during normal operations. Many programs, including DOS, use this command when storing temporary files.

The LOADHIGH command loads a program into higher memory.

The CD command (eg: CD\WINDOWS) changes the current directory to another. In the example, the CD\WINDOWS command changes the system to the WINDOWS directory.

The WIN command is the command to load Windows. It calls on the WIN.EXE file. If your system automatically comes up in Windows, the WIN command is more than likely a part of your AUTOEXEC.BAT file.

It is important to keep in mind that an incorrect statement or setting in either the CONFIG.SYS or the AUTOEXEC.BAT files can cause the system to fail or operate incorrectly.

If changes are required to the CONFIG.SYS or AUTOEXEC.BAT files, you can use the EDIT command to make them. EDIT is a line editor program that allows you to examine the current state of these files and, if necessary, add or remove the command lines. We recommend that if you edit these files, you make a backup copy of them first. This way, if something goes wrong, you can at least get back to where you started. Save the file as CONFIG.OLD or AUTOEXEC.OLD. By using the OLD extension, you can distinguish between the copy on disk and the original file stored on the drive.

For software configuration tools and commands for Windows, see page 174.

 # Windows

Windows is a graphical user interface (GUI) that allows you to switch between multiple applications and transfer information between them.

In Windows, the computer screen is called the desktop and displays all your work in rectangular areas called Windows. Each window displays a certain application, such as word processing documents or an electronic spreadsheet. These can be arranged on your desktop just as you arrange things on your real desk.

Windows also comes with some useful accessory programs such as an appointment calendar, a calculator, and a notepad, to name a few. It also provides on-line help menus that give quick and concise how-to information. It is easy to understand why Windows has gained popularity.

Hardware components used with Windows and setup procedures

Windows can run in many different hardware environments; however, the ideal environment includes:

➤ MS-DOS version 3.1 or later

➤ A personal computer with an Intel 80386 or faster microprocessor

➤ Greater than 2MB of memory (2 is usually considered absolute minimum and 4, 8, and 16 are becoming more standard.)

➤ Hard disk drive greater than 100MB (Many Windows applications require 8–12MB of free space.)

➤ At least one floppy drive

➤ A video monitor supported by Windows (VGA or SVGA recommended)

➤ A printer that is supported by Windows (laser recommended)

➤ A mouse supported by Windows

➤ A Hayes-compatible modem for use with the Windows communication software

When installing Windows, start at the DOS prompt by typing the word "setup" and hitting the return key. The setup program guides you through the installation by first evaluating the existing hardware environment, then copying the essential Windows files onto the hard disk. Along the way, it will ask you to verify critical information and make changes as needed. The information requested during setup includes:

➤ The directory where you want to store Windows

➤ The type of computer you are using

➤ Type of video display

➤ Type of mouse or pointing device, if any

> Keyboard type (101 or 102, with extended functions, etc.) and language layout (English, Spanish, etc.)

> Type of network, if any

> Type of printer and which I/O port is being used for it

> Applications on hard disk that you want to run with Windows

After the preliminary installation, setup loads the Windows software, installs the remaining files, and offers some options. Setup can run later at any time, just as with any other Windows application. This allows you to review or change previous settings if you wish. You may want to review settings when the customer is experiencing a failure to print, for example. The failure may be caused by the end user's selecting the wrong printing device when in setup.

When Windows first starts, the Program Manager application is open on your desktop. The Program Manager is central to Windows, and allows you to organize your other applications into groups and to start using them. There are basic elements and skills you need to know when working in Windows.

Major system files of Windows/Windows configuration tools and commands

Windows uses initialization files that contain information that defines to Windows your software and hardware needs. Windows for Workgroups and Windows-based applications can use the information stored in initialization files to make their configurations meet your system's hardware needs and your preferences for the look and feel of the operating environment.

There are two standard Windows initialization files:

> WIN.INI, which primarily contains settings that Windows maintains to customize your Windows environment according to your preference for such things as color, "wall-papers," sounds, etc.

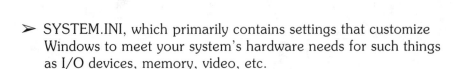

➤ SYSTEM.INI, which primarily contains settings that customize Windows to meet your system's hardware needs for such things as I/O devices, memory, video, etc.

There are two ways to change the WIN.INI settings:

➤ You can use the control panel to change most settings. This is the safest and recommended way because there is no need to open and edit the WIN.INI file, where it is easier to make mistakes.

➤ You can use a text editor, such as Notepad, to edit the WIN.INI file directly. This method is used to change settings that you cannot change through the control panel. Anytime the WIN.INI file is changed, you must restart Windows for the changes to take effect.

As with DOS and other operating systems, when you work with Windows, you'll need some knowledge of its general operation. It is beyond the scope of this book to teach you Windows; however, we do provide a Windows Basic Skills checklist identifying the areas you need to know in the service/repair environment. For additional reading and training on Windows, refer to Appendices C and D in the back of this book.

Windows basic skills checklist

In order to be considered proficient in Windows, you need a working knowledge of some basic skills. This is critical in a repair scenario so that you can navigate through the operating environment. As you review the following checklist, compare it with what you already know of the Windows operating environment.

➤ Types of Windows
  • Application
  • Document

➤ Parts of a Window
  • Control-menu box
  • Window corner
  • Workspace

- Selection cursor
- Mouse pointer
- Title bar
- Window title
- Window border
- Menu bar
- Scroll bars horizontal and vertical
- Maximize and Minimum buttons

➤ Icons
- Application icons
- Document icons
- Program item icons

➤ Working with menus
- Selecting and canceling
- Choosing menu commands
- Using control menus

➤ Working with dialog boxes
- Moving dialog boxes
- Choosing options
- Closing a dialog box

➤ Working with a window
- Moving windows
- Changing the size of a window
- Closing a window

➤ Working with applications
- Running two or more applications
- Switching between applications
- Arranging application windows

➤ Working with documents
- Opening and saving documents/files
- Switching and arranging document windows
- Working with text
- Using on-line help functions
- Starting help
- Using help
- Finding information in help

➢ Control panel
  • Desktop options
  • Installing and configuring printers
  • Connection to network printers
  • Removing an installed printer
  • Configuring communication ports
  • Setting network options

➢ CONFIG.SYS file command lines
  • HIMEM.SYS (extended memory manager)
  • SMARTDrive (disk caching program)
  • RAMDrive (to set up a RAM disk)
  • EMM386.SYS (expanded memory emulator)

Windows 95

Two of the main goals in the development of Windows 95 are discussed hereafter:

➢ Support of the plug-and-play standard

➢ Ease of installation and configuration on existing Windows 3.1 installations

Plug-and-play support

"Plug-and-play" is a standard being developed by Microsoft, Intel, Phoenix Technologies, and others. Its intent is to allow for easy installations, easy reconfiguration, and quick on-the-fly configuration changes for any peripheral device that meets the standard. In order for this standard to be successful, it must have the cooperation of the operating system supplier, system manufacturers, BIOS developers, and device vendors. By working together, these industry players are contributing common user interfaces, along with common device drivers, installation procedures, and other features helpful to the user.

To fully understand how plug-and-play is implemented in Windows 95, it is important to understand the various elements of the subsystem. They are the hardware tree, INF files, registry, events, and the configuration manager.

The hardware tree is the database of information that describes the current system configuration. It is built by the configuration manager and stored in memory.

INF files are a collection of disk files that contain information about particular types of devices. For example, SCSI.INF contains information about every known SCSI device. When a new SCSI device is installed, a new .INF file is created specific to that new device.

The registry is a database maintained by Windows 95 for storing hardware and software configuration information.

Events are a set of application programming interfaces (APIs) used to signal changes in the system's current configuration.

The configuration manager is the central component supporting the Plug-and-play capability. It builds into the registry the database of information describing the machine's configuration, and notifies device drivers of their assigned resources.

Ease of installation and configuration on existing Windows 3.1 installations

An easy installation requires no more than swapping diskettes. Windows 95 can use the configuration information from the previous Windows installation for the new setup. Instead of lengthy INI files that many of us are familiar with from earlier versions of Windows, Windows 95 uses the registry mentioned above. Entries in the registry are available to application programs through APIs (application programming interfaces). Applications can add to and retrieve their private configuration settings using registry access APIs. This registry cannot be edited by the user, so no inconsistencies can be introduced.

Some of the major features in Windows 95 are as follows:

> ➤ It presents its own interface to support electronic mail.

> ➤ Long filenames are no longer limited to the standard 8 characters.

> File viewers allow you to examine a formatted file without having access to the application that created it. For example, it allows you to view a file created with DBase 2, even if you don't have that application loaded.

> Support for Pen systems such as those used in the mobile marketplace on systems such as Apple Newton.

> Better support for MS-DOS applications. Even though it is not an MS-DOS environment, Windows 95 performs well with applications written specifically for DOS.

> Easier System administration and reconfiguration procedures.

Every aspect of the existing system was analyzed to improve ease of installation and upgrading. You should not be confused when adding any new device to the Windows 95 environment.

 # Installing and upgrading

 ## Upgrade potential and component compatibility

As you add new components to the system, such as more RAM, or a different video board or monitor, you will be required to make changes to some of the files. This ensures that the system has all the information needed to work with the total hardware environment, and that the system is optimized for maximum performance. The greatest hardware environment, if not configured properly, will run slowly.

But before beginning any upgrade or installation, it is important to review both the current and the proposed hardware and/or software environment. Is it just a hardware installation, just a software installation, or both? If you are not sure what is to be done, you cannot know if you have everything necessary for successful completion. You need to know at the start if all the elements that must work together after the upgrade or installation are software compatible as well as physically and electrically compatible.

For example, it may seem like a good idea to upgrade your VGA video board to an SVGA card. But will the current video display support the new card, or will that have to be upgraded also? Do you have enough available hard drive space for the new software package you plan to add? Do you have enough RAM to support the new environment you're creating?

All too often, technicians return to a system two or three times before they have all these questions answered. It's better to answer them all at the start. We also recommend that you don't rely on customers to tell you what they need. If they ask you to install more memory, you might want to ask why. Make sure that adding memory will really give the customer the benefit he or she wants. Too often customers add memory and expect great improvements in performance only to be disappointed by the results.

Common drivers:
function and configuration

Each of the computer's hardware components is called a device and has characteristics that can be customized by using commands in the config.sys file. For example, you could change the language designation of the keyboard from English to French or Spanish.

MS-DOS uses a program called a device driver to control every device. There are device drivers for your keyboard, hard disk, floppy disk, and I/O ports. Because these device drivers are built-in, you do not have to do anything special to use them.

Some common drivers are:

> ➢ ANSI.SYS
> ➢ DISPLAY.SYS
> ➢ DRIVER.SYS
> ➢ EMM386.EXE
> ➢ HIMEM.SYS
> ➢ RAMDRIVE.SYS

ANSI.SYS supports American National Standards Institute (ANSI) terminal emulation.

DISPLAY.SYS supports high-speed page switching for monitors.

DRIVER.SYS allocates a portion of memory to be used or designated as a logical device.

EMM386.EXE simulates expanded memory and provides access to the upper memory area on a computer with an 80386 or higher processor with extended memory.

HIMEM.SYS manages the use of extended memory on a computer with an 80286 or higher processor and extended memory.

RAMDRIVE.SYS simulates a hard disk drive by creating a virtual disk drive in the system's RAM.

Methods for upgrading DOS

The easiest way to perform any upgrade of MS-DOS is to use the automatic installation and upgrade utility that is built into DOS. By swapping disks as instructed by the utility, you replace the existing version files with the new version.

Another process that could be performed when upgrading is the re-partitioning of the hard drive. The hard drive can be partitioned to represent many different logical "devices" (drives). Partitioning dates back to the early days of PCs, when MS-DOS had the capability to recognize a maximum of 32MB for any given logical drive or partition. A 50MB drive might have been partitioned into two sections, and DOS would see those partitions as drive C and drive D.

A disk may still need to be partitioned today—not to divide it into multiple devices, but, as mentioned earlier, to make the hard drive as a whole capable of accepting information.

In today's software environment there is rarely a need to partition the hard drive unless you are configuring a hard drive for the first time that has never been partitioned before.

However, if you do repartition any hard drive that has been partitioned before and has data on it, it is important to first back up all data on the drive to avoid losing it.

Windows installation

✳ Methods for installing andupgrading Windows

To install Windows for the very first time, place the Windows installation disk #1 in floppy drive A.

At the A> prompt, type setup and press Enter.

You will be asked if you want to perform an Express Setup or a Custom Setup. Unless you are experienced with the Custom Setup, choose Express Setup.

Setup checks the configuration of your system, then asks you on which directory of the hard drive you want Windows installed. The default is C:\WINDOWS; however, you can select any directory you wish.

Setup begins copying files to the hard disk and prompts you along the way to insert the next installation disk, until all files have been loaded. During this process, the Windows installation program brings up screens explaining various features and benefits of the Windows environment that you're installing, and gives you a chance to register your software.

At the end of installation, you will be prompted to choose a printer type. If you do not choose one, Windows will not set up any printer driver for you. A new printer driver can always be selected later.

After selecting your printer, Windows begins searching your hard drive for all application programs and sets up DOS path statements and an icon for each one that it can identify. (Clicking on that icon thereafter will prompt the system to locate and activate that program.) For those

applications that the system cannot identify, Windows asks you to assign a name to each one for which it builds a DOS path statement and icon.

The last thing Windows prompts you for is whether you want to run a short tutorial on Windows. You can always go back later and run the tutorial at a later session.

When you install Windows for the first time, the first part of the Setup program runs in MS-DOS. Setup switches into the Windows mode and presents you with a Windows interface offering point-and-click options.

If Setup stops, or locks up while in the MS-DOS mode, it may be because it couldn't identify some system hardware and therefore didn't know what to do with it. To solve this problem, type SETUP/I at the DOS prompt. This will skip hardware detection and run Custom Setup.

In the system information screen, be sure to select descriptions that match the hardware on your system: for example, VGA video, 486 processor, and 500MB hard drive.

One feature of Windows that allows for easy installation of application programs is its standardization of many common commands, such as SETUP. To install any program designed to run with Windows, from the Program Manager select FILE, then RUN, and type in A:\SETUP. From that point onward, you will be instructed when to change disks or enter information.

qThe preceding description of the Windows installation is the same for all versions. However, when you install Windows for Workgroups, you are also prompted to supply information about the network you have installed.

Diagnosing software problems

This section is concerned primarily with diagnosing software problems. For more materials on diagnosing hardware problems, see Chapter 4's diagnosing section.

 # System boot sequences/approaches to diagnosing

Earlier in the chapter, we looked at the hierarchy of the system software, from the ROM BIOS to the application programs, and examined the three main files necessary to make a disk bootable (IO.SYS, MSDOS.SYS, and COMMAND.COM). This information is important to the topic of diagnosing. You need to know how systems operate in order to successfully diagnose problems.

Problems in the microcomputer environment occur in four areas:

> ➤ Hardware

> ➤ Software

> ➤ Environment

> ➤ Operator Error

You should know how to distinguish between software and hardware errors. The quickest, most efficient way is to have with you disk-based diagnostics for identifying hardware problems, and a copy of DOS. Remember to use your own software—the customer's AUTOEXEC.BAT and CONFIG.SYS files may be defective.

Here's a true story that illustrates the helpfulness of bringing your own software with you to the customer site:

A customer began to get error messages saying "insufficient memory" when he tried to run a word processor. The first step the technician took was to run some memory disk-based diagnostics. From his initial conversation with the user, he knew that the memory errors occurred during the loading of that one word processor program; however, he still wanted to be sure of memory integrity.

After a complete test of the memory circuits revealed no errors, the technician loaded a copy of DOS from his floppy disks. With that loaded, he logged over to the hard drive directory that contained the word processor and executed the command file to load that program. The word processor loaded without fail and executed flawlessly.

At this point, the technician examined the CONFIG.SYS and AUTOEXEC.BAT files. The CONFIG.SYS was in order, but the AUTOEXEC.BAT file had an unusually large number of memory-resident programs. The customer had received some public domain pop-up programs and wanted them all. The programs took up so much memory that not enough was left when the customer attempted to run the word processor, hence the "insufficient memory" error messages. By having his own software, the technician saved time in isolating the cause of the problem.

If you do not have your own copy of DOS, you could rename the user's AUTOEXEC.BAT and CONFIG.SYS files temporarily, so that they don't execute upon start-up. (Those files are not needed for boot-up.) If the system works without those files, but not with them, it's a good sign that they are causing the problem.

These techniques apply to all areas of the operating environment. If a port does not print or receive data, copies of your own software could assist in finding this out. For example, if you boot up in the customer's software environment, and the system will not print, but when you boot up with your own software, the system does print; then, most likely, files in the customer's system have been misconfigured or damaged. But be careful not to modify anything within the customer's operating system environment until you are sure it is the solution to the problem.

The software you will want to have with you includes disk-based diagnostics, an operating environment (such as MS-DOS or Windows), a simple application program familiar to you, and a current virus-scan application. (You do not want to be accused of transferring viruses to your customer's equipment.)

It is generally a good idea to carry more than one copy of any disk-based diagnostic because at times a copy might become corrupted. If a floppy disk drive corrupts your disk, you should have another available.

The methods required to solve and repair software problems are very simple and straightforward. First determine whether the problem is hardware- or software-related. As with any problem, you need to consider all the aspects of the software and hardware that are

involved. For example, let us assume that a customer is having difficulty printing from a word processor. First look at all the areas that could possibly cause the problem:

➤ Serial and/or parallel port

➤ Software application

➤ Cabling

➤ Printer

➤ Power

➤ Operator error

✳ Questions to ask about customer problems

Some questions you might ask the operator in the above example:

➤ Does the error occur throughout all applications or with one particular application?

➤ Is the error intermittent or consistent?

➤ What error messages, if any, were displayed?

➤ Can the operator recreate the error?

➤ Can you continue after the error, or is the machine locked up?

➤ Is the printer plugged in and loaded with paper?

➤ Is the Windows print manager configured properly?

➤ Is all cabling in order?

➤ Does the printer successfully perform its self-test?

Questions like these will either quickly identify the cause of the problem or send you on to run diagnostics on the system. Take each challenge step by step.

Many software-related errors are caused by configuration errors. People inadvertently modify or change a setting without realizing it. When investigating any problem, leave no stone unturned. You will, however, face some situations that escape explanation.

Correcting the problem generally requires you to have access to the master diskettes or a current backup for the system. This is necessary

to obtain specific device drivers. Always refer to the software documentation, if available.

 # Common DOS failures

A failure means that, for some reason, during execution, the desired action or results were not accomplished. A failure could be caused by corruption of the operating system (which is software code), by a hardware failure, or by an external influence (magnetic fields, heat, etc.). The failure might even be caused by operator error.

Today, because of graphic-user interface environments like Windows, we meet fewer problems caused by operator error than we did in the days of working from the DOS prompt. For example, today's "Bad command or file name" error message usually means that the file is not on the disk drive, nor in the directory that the command line specified it would be in.

Some common error messages include:

➤ *Bad command or file name.* This message comes up because DOS could not locate the file. In some cases, the problem may be an input error by the operator.

➤ *Error reading drive.* There are a host of messages describing the system's inability to read a diskette or hard drive. The error may stem from anything involved with the read operation. Possibilities include a corrupted disk, an unformatted disk drive, or no diskette in the drive, as well as software errors. The system may be having problems reading only a single file, but gives a message saying it is unable to read the drive that the file is on.

➤ *Not enough memory.* A message of this nature indicates that the system attempted to load a file or program but had insufficient memory available to do so. This message is common today because many programs require far more memory than in the past. Users also sometimes overload their systems with memory-resident programs, leaving insufficient memory to run application programs.

➤ *Unable to load device driver.* This message indicates that the system attempted to load a device driver, but the device could not be found. This message could apply to drivers for any device, such as the mouse, memory driver, or network card. Questions to ask yourself are: Was the device attached? Has the device failed? Has the correct driver been selected for loading the device?

Regardless of the problems you encounter, it is important to know what the computer was attempting to do at the time of error. Common sense will help you from there. If you were attempting to read a disk, don't go looking for errors in the AUTOEXEC.BAT file.

 # Common Windows failures

There are a number of errors that can be encountered in the Windows environment. Even simple installations can run into glitches. Remember that if your installation falters, it could be due to an inability of the system to recognize the hardware. Type SETUP/I at the DOS prompt to skip hardware detection and run custom setup.

If you have completed setup and Windows will not start, one of the following may be the cause:

➤ The wrong hardware may have been specified for the system during a custom setup.

➤ The computer may not be running on the required microprocessor—at least a 386SX microprocessor—or it may not have enough memory to support your version of Windows (Windows 3.1, Windows for Workgroups 3.11, or Windows NT).

➤ The computer system may be running memory-resident (terminal stay resident) programs that are incompatible with Windows and could not be detected during setup. To check this possibility, create a "clean boot" floppy disk that contains only the files necessary to start the computer and Windows. Boot this "clean copy" from the floppy drive. If Windows starts, the system is probably running memory-resident programs incompatible with Windows.

➤ If you are using Windows for Workgroups and using a network card, be sure that all network connections are intact.

If, after checking all of the above, Windows still will not start, try the following:

➤ If this is Windows for Workgroups and a network is involved, start Windows by typing WIN/N at the DOS prompt to start Windows without starting the network. If this command is successful in starting Windows, contact the network administrator to investigate problems on the network.

➤ Start Windows by typing WIN/B at the DOS prompt. This creates a file, BOOTLOG.TXT, that records system messages generated during system start-up. By using the MS-DOS type command, you can view this file to see where in the start-up process Windows failed. In MS-DOS versions 5.0 or later, use the edit command instead of type.

➤ In the Windows for Workgroups environment, use the EMMExclude option when you start Windows, by typing WIN/D:X at the DOS prompt. This option excludes the network interface card from areas that Windows searches for unused address space. (Typically, this is the area A000-FFFF.) The search can cause conflicts with adapters that use this area.

Repairing

Other materials on repairing hardware and software problems appear in Chapter 4. See that chapter's sections on diagnosing and repairing.

Replacing hardware

If, after diagnosing the problem, you learn that the cause was hardware-related, you will be faced with having to choose and swap a module. When removing any module always adhere to ESD standards and practices. (These are discussed in Chapter 4, on page 85.) Failure to follow these practices may result in either immediate component failure or deterioration and, later, premature failure of the component.

Once you have handled the hardware issues, you can correct software errors by changing configuration settings, including a wrong choice of

device driver, or by reloading the software. If there is a current backup of the system, you may also need to reload it.

 # Solving software problems

Eliminate the obvious. If your printer is not functioning, you can safely assume that your video drivers are not the cause of the problem.

Experience the error. Can you recreate the error and see what happens when the error occurs?

Ask questions. Is the problem application-specific, or could it be related to either your DOS or Windows environments? Ask questions!

Fix it. Replace that driver, reload that application, edit the CONFIG.SYS, or whatever else it takes to bring this system back on line.

Take it step by step and you will not miss.

 # Sample test questions

What follows are sample test questions and answers for the Microsoft Windows/DOS specialty exam. Each sample test question in this chapter comes from one of the same three sources as the test questions at the end of Chapter 4 (Self Test Software, CompTIA, or the authors), and all credits are similarly given. See page 152 in Chapter 4 for more information about these sources.

1. Is it necessary to have WINA20.386 in the root directory to run Windows 3.1 in the enhanced mode? *(Self Test Software)*
   a. No, it may be removed.
   b. No, it may be moved to another directory.
   c. Yes, WINA20.386 must be in the root directory.
   d. Yes, WINA20.386 is required in any subdirectory.

2. After replacing a hard drive, you try to format it and get a message that says "Invalid media type." What should you do? *(Self Test Software)*
   a. Run the diagnostics.
   b. Run FDISK.

    c. Run MEDIA.COM.

    d. RUN CHKDSK.

3. For a hard drive to boot Microsoft MS-DOS, which of the following files must be present? Choose all that apply. *(Self Test Software)*

    a. IO.SYS

    b. MSDOS.SYS

    c. COMMAND.COM

    d. CONFIG.SYS

4. The DOS command "FORMAT A:/S" will cause which of the following? Choose all that apply. *(Self Test Software)*

    a. Format the diskette in the A: drive.

    b. Make the diskette in the A: drive bootable.

    c. Create a subdirectory on the diskette in the A: drive.

    d. Save existing files on the diskette in the A: drive.

5. Which of the following files is used to customize the Windows environment? *(Self Test Software)*

    a. WIN.INI

    b. SYSTEM.INI

    c. SETUP.INI

    d. CONFIG.SYS

6. Which of the following files is used to load a memory manager? *(Self Test Software)*

    a. AUTOEXEC.BAT

    b. CONFIG.SYS

    c. COMMAND.COM

    d. MSDOS.SYS

7. Which of the following commands would NOT be found in the AUTOEXEC.BAT file? *(Self Test Software)*

    a. Path=C:\

    b. Echo off

    c. Device=HIMEM.SYS

    d. Prompt pg

8. The Windows command SETUP/I will do what? *(Self Test Software)*

    a. Search for incompatible software.

    b. Ignore automatic hardware detection.

    c. Begin administrative setup.

    d. Display information about setup.

9. Which of the following commands are found in the CONFIG.SYS file? Choose all that apply. *(Self Test Software)*
   a. Echo on.
   b. Buffers.
   c. Break.
   d. Device.

10. What is the FIRST step when installing a new DOS upgrade? *(Self Test Software)*
    a. Delete the COMMAND.COM file.
    b. Back up the existing operating system and data.
    c. Reformat the currently formatted hard drive.
    d. Copy the previous version of the operating system to a subdirectory called OLD_DOS.

11. Which of the following is the correct procedure to install a Windows program? *(Self Test Software)*
    a. Type RUN from the DOS prompt, then enter the install program name.
    b. Click on File, then Star, then enter the install program name.
    c. Click on File, then Run, then enter the program name.
    d. None of the above.

12. When you begin to diagnose a computer problem, what is the best way to differentiate between a hardware and a software problem? *(CompTIA)*
    a. Upgrade the operating system.
    b. Format drive C: and reload software.
    c. Replace the system board.
    d. Boot from a "clean boot" diskette.

13. How much memory does DOS real mode require? *(Self Test Software)*
    a. 640K.
    b. 1024K.
    c. 2048K.
    d. 4096K.

14. To make a program launch automatically immediately after Windows initializes, _____. Choose all that apply. *(CompTIA)*
    a. Add its name to the AUTO= line in the WIN.INI file.
    b. Add its icon to the STARTUP program group.
    c. Add its name to the RUN= line in the WIN.INI file.

d. Add its icon to the AUTOEXE program group.

e. Add its name to the LOAD= line in the WIN.INI file.

15. Which of the following interprets the input entered at the DOS prompt? *(Self Test Software)*

a. COMMAND.COM

b. IBMBIO.COM

c. IBMDOS.COM

d. CONFIG.SYS

16. How many bytes are usually stored on a hard drive sector running DOS? *(Self Test Software)*

a. 512

b. 1024

c. 512K

d. 1024K

17. When adding a second hard drive, who determines the drive letter? *(Self Test Software)*

a. The end user.

b. The drive manufacturer.

c. DOS.

d. SETUP utility.

18. Which function key will retrieve the last input from the DOS command prompt? *(Self Test Software)*

a. F1

b. F2

c. F3

d. F4

19. A system will boot from a diskette but not from the hard drive. Which of the following should you do? Choose all that apply. *(Self Test Software)*

a. Verify that the two hidden files are present.

b. Verify that COMMAND.COM is present.

c. Replace the hard drive.

d. Format the hard drive.

20. Which file contains the commands that configure a computer's hardware components? *(CompTIA)*

a. CONFIG.SYS

b. DOSSHELL.EXE

    c. SETVER.EXE
    d. COMMAND.COM

21. Which of the following is an incorrect entry for the CONFIG.SYS file? *(Self Test Software)*
    a. DEVICE=ANSI.SYS
    b. DEVICE=HIMEM.SYS
    c. DEVICE=MOUSE.COM
    d. DEVICE=EMM386.EXE

22. Which of the following file extensions are executable from the DOS command prompt? Choose all that apply. *(Self Test Software)*
    a. .BAT
    b. .EXE
    c. .SYS
    d. .COM

23. Which of the following statements describes the DOS=HIGH? Choose all that apply. *(Self Test Software)*
    a. Loads the DOS kernel between the addresses 1024 and 1088.
    b. Provides additional conventional memory.
    c. Loads the DOS kernel in HMA.
    d. Frees up extended memory.

24. In which of the following is KEYBOARD.SYS found? *(Self Test Software)*
    a. CONFIG.SYS
    b. AUTOEXEC.BAT
    c. INSTALL.BAT
    d. SETUP.EXE

⇨ Answers to the sample questions

1. A	7. C	13. A	19. A, B
2. B	8. B	14. B, C, E	20. A
3. A, B, C	9. B, C, D	15. A	21. C
4. A, B	10. B	16. A	22. A, B, D
5. A	11. C	17. C	23. A, B, C
6. B	12. D	18. C	24. A

The Macintosh OS-based computers exam

THE specific skills and knowledge that are tested on the Macintosh OS-based computers specialty exam are listed below. Each skill or knowledge is covered in the preparatory materials that follow. We have also presented additional topics where we felt these would be helpful. If upon reviewing a section of this, or the other study guide chapters, you feel a need for more information, please refer to Appendices C and D for recommended sources of further reading and training.

Note that for the Macintosh OS-based computers specialty exam, Sylvan Prometric has identified the topic areas of installing and upgrading, and repair as the two areas in which test candidates have the most difficulty. Be sure to concentrate your preparation in these areas.

This chapter concludes with sample questions and answers to help you prepare for the Macintosh OS-based computers specialty exam.

The exam tests your ability to do the following:

➢ Content area one: Configuring
  • Identify significant hardware differences between Macintosh systems (for instance, Quadra versus Power Macintosh, modular versus compact models).
  • Sequence the steps required for setting up Macintosh system hardware, including peripheral devices.
  • Determine the appropriate functions and commands to initialize and copy (back up) selected media types such as hard disk, removable hard disks, floppy disks, etc.
  • Identify steps required to upgrade a Macintosh system including RAM, drives, cards.
  • List key elements which must be checked in "Chooser" after changing a configuration.
  • Sequence the steps required for installing Macintosh system software.
  • Specify proper utilities and system tools to use during Macintosh hardware and software setup (including Installer, Disk Tools, etc.).
  • Identify steps required to perform a "clean install" of the Macintosh operating system.
  • Identify steps required to connect to a network and to verify successful connection.

> Content area two: Installing and upgrading
  - Describe the functions of various steps in the system start-up sequence.
  - Identify the major components of the Macintosh operating system and their functions.
  - Identify common inits and extensions and their functions.
  - For the Macintosh operating system, identify various special boot procedures and when to use them.
  - Identify differences in features and functions between the different versions of the Macintosh OS (System 6 and later).
  - Identify common commands used in Macintosh applications.
  - Identify major features of the Macintosh desktop and their functions.

> Content area three: Diagnosis
  - Identify the common questions that should be asked when determining a customer's system problem.
  - Identify steps and/or tools required to isolate software problems.
  - Identify the visual and audio indicators of common system malfunctions.
  - Identify the likely meaning of common error codes, start-up messages and icons from the boot sequence, and identify the course of action required to correct a start-up error.
  - Know when to use Apple HDSC Setup, Disk First Aid, and other Apple utilities needed to format and/or test and repair hard drives.

> Content area four: Repair
  - Identify the correct modules, components, or utilities required to repair a given problem.

Configuring

Macintosh system hardware

Several product lines comprise the Macintosh family of computers. These are the Power Macs, Quadras, LCs, Performas, and Powerbooks (see Figs. 6-1, 6-2, and 6-3). Even though these product

Figure 6-1

A Power Macintosh 9500. Apple Computer, Inc., 1995. All rights reserved. Used with permission.

Figure 6-2

A Power Macintosh 7200/90. Apple Computer, Inc., 1995. All rights reserved. Used with permission.

Figure 6-3

A Powerbook 5300, 2300, and 190.

lines include several models, you will find that many of the technological features of these models are the same.

Each of the product lines listed is targeted toward a particular specialty market. The markets include business, educational, home/consumer, and mobile. Power Macs and Quadras are for the business community and include much of the new technology such as desktop video, voice recognition, and the ability to run PC software.

Power Macs differ from Quadras on the kind of processor technology used. Quadras run on the 68040 processor chip, while the Power Macs use the Power PC, the latest RISC (reduced instruction set computer) technology.

The LCs and Performas are low to medium performance computer systems in terms of memory, speed, and technical complexity. The Performas are targeted to the home/consumer market, and the LCs to the educational market. Powerbooks are portable, battery-operated Macintoshes designed for those who require a system to travel with. Powerbooks are similar in performance to the Performas and LCs. They typically cost more, although price varies depending on the screen installed.

The Apple Macintosh computer system comes in compact and modular versions. The compact version has an all-in-one display

setup; the modular version has a separate video display. Installing or setting up each version is similar, except for the video. In the modular version, you may need to install an optional video card, depending on the monitor used.

After unpacking the various models, you'll need to connect cables. On the compact models, you need to connect the power cord, keyboard, and mouse. With the modular versions, you have to connect the power cord, video card, keyboard, mouse, and display monitor.

When working with Quadra computers, do not plug in the power cord until all NuBus expansion cards have been installed. If there is power to the logic board, damage could result to the expansion cards. As with any computer system, it is wise to cut power when connecting or disconnecting cabling.

Macintosh systems differ on performance, peripheral support, and expandability. Many hardware components can affect performance, including the microprocessor and clock, the co-processor, memory caches, hard drives, and CD-ROMs. Peripheral support includes items such as video monitor support, networking capability, sound/voice recognition, motion video, and phone/fax features. The following supported ports might be on your Mac, depending on the model:

➢ Modem

➢ Printer

➢ SCSI

➢ Ethernet

➢ Display

➢ ADB (Apple desktop bus)

➢ Sound input

➢ Sound output

➢ Video input

➢ Video output

➢ Headphone

➢ Floppy drive

Expandability depends upon the type of slots available for expansion cards and the type of bays available for disk drive or CD-ROM upgrades. The type and number of slots vary from Mac to Mac, and there are two basic types of slots: Nubus and processor-direct slots (PDS). See Fig. 6-4.

Figure 6-4

An inside view of a Macintosh.

After all components have been connected, verify the connections with those outlined in any installation/user's manual, then turn on power. If the machine does not power up properly, promptly cut power and refer to the troubleshooting section of the documentation supplied.

⇨ Initializing hard disk and floppy media

Most systems come with an initialized hard drive pre-loaded with software. It is extremely important, however, to know how to format a drive should it be needed after a major hardware or software failure. Apple provides a program called HDSC Setup for formatting Apple hard drives. If you use third-party drives, they must be formatted with the utility software that comes with the drive.

If there are any external hard drives to connect, this is done through the SCSI (small computer systems interface), commonly referred to as "scuzzy." The Power Mac series has two SCSI buses built in. To connect the first external drive (more than one may be connected) you must use a system cable. This cable has a 25-pin connector on one end and a 50-pin connector on the other. It connects the first peripheral in the SCSI chain to the Macintosh Computer.

If you are connecting more than one external, you must use a peripheral interface cable between the drives. This cable has a 50-pin connector at both ends. There is also a cable extender available; however, no SCSI chain should be greater than 20 feet. Some important things to remember when positioning the external hard drives or any other SCSI devices, such as CD-ROM drives, printers, and scanners around the Mac:

➤ Do not block any air vents.

➤ Always place the drive right side up and not on its side.

➤ Do not place the drive to the left of a compact computer, because the left side contains circuitry that forms a magnetic field and could interfere with the hard drive.

➤ Terminators are needed to ensure signal integrity along a SCSI bus. Improper termination, or no termination at all, will cause SCSI system problems.

➤ Any device in a SCSI chain that is terminated (usually the first and last) must be powered on in order to pass information along the chain. Devices in the middle may be powered off.

➤ The SCSI port will support a maximum of eight devices. The computer itself and the internal hard drive both count as a SCSI device, which leaves you a maximum of six external devices that can be added. The Macintosh system is always assigned a SCSI ID of 7, and the internal hard drive is assigned number 0.

In some cases where the internal drive will not start up the system, it may be necessary to start up from an external hard drive. To bypass the internal hard drive, turn on the computer, or choose restart from the special menu, and hold down the command, option, shift, and

delete keys. When the LED on the external hard drive blinks on and off a few times, release the keys.

The first time a new floppy disk is inserted into a Macintosh floppy drive, a dialog box may tell you that the disk is unreadable. If it is a brand new disk and never been used, this is the expected message. If the disk contains information, or you thought it did, there could be a problem with that diskette.

Another message you may see with a previously formatted disk tells you that the diskette is not a Macintosh disk. This will usually indicate to you that the disk has been formatted in another OS environment or that it is corrupted.

In any case, if the disk is brand new, it needs to be formatted. In the dialog box that indicated the disk was unreadable, it also asks you if you wish to initialize it. After pointing and clicking on the initialize box, you will then be given one more opportunity to change your mind. (Macintosh operating systems are very forgiving.) You will also have the ability to name the disk. If no name is given, the disk will be labeled "untitled."

When working with any Macintosh system, it is always important to have some emergency recovery tools available. In the event that the hard drive does not boot, you will need to have a "bootable" floppy disk to bring the system up. Your Disk Tools disk will perform this function, just make sure that the floppy disk is write-protected so that no damage could occur to that disk. Once the system is booted, you will be able to see if you can access the hard drive. Sometimes system files get corrupted, preventing the system from booting, and yet the application files are intact.

Keep in mind that it is important to prepare for an emergency. Too many times, computer users will realize what they should have done when it is too late.

Upgrading Macintosh systems

When planning any type of upgrade, carefully consider the kind of performance increase you can expect. Even though you may be

upgrading the processor, the computer will not necessarily perform like a later model Mac because of other improvements made in late-model bus structures and internal system communications. Always consider the cost of the alternatives. It may be more economical to improve system performance by replacing the entire machine with a later model.

The upgrades that could be considered for a Mac include:

> Processor

> Co-processors

> Logic board

> Clock boosters

> Serial ports

> Expansion slots

Processor replacements come in various forms; some use processor direct slots, others plug into the original CPU socket, and still others just clip to the legs of the existing processor.

Co-processors are generally used for high-end mathematical computations and will only work with application software that has been designed to use them. Simply speaking, if you add a co-processor and your software does not call on it, the chip is doing nothing but drawing power and providing heat, with no effect on system performance.

Replacing the logic board usually means trying to connect as many components as possible from your original system to a new main logic board. These components include, among others, power supplies, disk drives, and modems.

Clock boosters are upgrades that change the original clock crystal to a faster one. This is useful as long as the other circuitry in the machine has the capability to handle it. Otherwise, it is like putting a super charger on an old engine. If the engine is not set up to handle that additional chamber pressure, you will overtax the engine and destroy it. Similarly, if you change inputs in the computer faster than the chips can respond to them, you tax the computer beyond its capability to

respond in a proper time and manner. The result, over time, is a breakdown in the operation of computer components.

Most Macs come with two serial ports. In the event that you require more, a number of third-party companies offer options for enhancement. One way to increase the serial port capacity is to add a switching box to the port, so that it can work with two devices (not, however, at the same time). The other method is to add an expansion card that plugs into a Nubus slot and gives you two or more serial ports.

Expansion slots can be added with other third-party add-ons. In many cases, these upgrades will include a separate enclosure with its own power supply that interconnects to your Mac.

Often, the need for memory causes us to upgrade our existing configuration. This upgrading process varies from model to model. For example, in the Powerbook series there is only one memory upgrade slot, so if you install a 4-megabyte (MB) upgrade, and need more later, you will have to replace it, not just add to it. This kind of restriction happens in a laptop or portable environment because manufacturers are faced with a limited amount of machine space.

In the desktop models of the Macintosh, you will find additional SIMMs (single in-line memory module) slots available for additional memory module plug-in. SIMMs come in sizes from 256 kilobytes to 16MB, in pin counts from 30 to 72, and in memory speeds of 150 nanoseconds to 60 nanoseconds access time.

With memory, it is critical to be aware of which Mac environment you are working with and the amount of total memory that environment will support. Please refer to the system documentation for this information.

The Chooser utility

When setting up your printer or changing the printer that you are using, it will be necessary to use a utility called the Chooser. Chooser allows you to select the type of printer you will be using and ensures that the proper device driver software is implemented. Chooser manages the collection of device drivers for the various printers, and

some device drivers will come with a third-party printer made for the Macintosh environment.

Printer drivers go into the extension folder of your system folder; however, from the group of printer drivers, you still need to choose the one you will use. This is where Chooser comes into play. Normally, you select Chooser from the menu and click on the printer you want.

If you change printers during a session, you need to be certain that the selected printer has changed for any open applications. To make sure this takes place, open the applications page setup dialog box and then close it again.

 # Macintosh system software

As with all computer systems, Macintosh computers adhere to a standard hierarchy of software. That hierarchy is:

> ➤ ROM

> ➤ Operating system (within the system folder)

> ➤ Application software (spreadsheets, word processor, etc.)

Macintosh system software has gone through many revisions. System software is usually revised in order to work with new hardware technology or to correct errors in earlier systems or ROM versions. Even though the system cannot write corrections to ROM, it can store the changes in RAM when the system loads.

System software on Macintosh computers comes pre-loaded from the factory, but there might be times when you will have to reload some of the software. These times could include:

> ➤ When upgrading to a new version

> ➤ After installing a new hard drive

> ➤ After file corruption by viruses or other external influences including hardware and software corruption

> ➤ When performing system maintenance

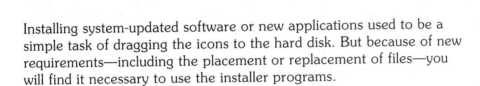

Installing system-updated software or new applications used to be a simple task of dragging the icons to the hard disk. But because of new requirements—including the placement or replacement of files—you will find it necessary to use the installer programs.

These installer programs—which come with Apple systems and even with applications programs—contain scripts written by the developers that specify where to place what files, depending on the type of Mac system. Although some find the installers unnecessary, it is usually best to let the installers do the major portion of the work.

Many third-party companies use Apple's installer. However, with the variety of installer programs in the marketplace, you will find some that differ in process and procedures.

In order to run System 7 software, you will need the following hardware:

- ➤ Mac with SCSI hard disk
- ➤ 4MB of RAM (8MB if Power Mac)

The System 7 operating system requires anywhere from 7MB to 15MB of hard drive space for installation. In most cases, all you have to do to install system software is to double-click on the installer icon on your system software disks and follow the instructions on the screen. You may also use custom installation, which will allow you to clean up corrupted files or just to install certain capabilities of the system.

You must have System 7 on diskette or CD, or have it available through the network. Keep in mind that the installer utility makes a copy of your system folder then makes changes to the copy. At the end of the installation it "approves" the copied folder and removes the original. This is why additional disk space is required for installation.

Before installing the System 7 environment, you will need to do the following:

- ➤ Calculate available memory with MultiFinder, which was an option under System 6, but is now a feature under System 7. MultiFinder runs each application in its own memory partition. Keep in mind that memory can become fragmented when you

open several applications. Fragmented memory can be recovered by closing all applications and restarting them.

➢ Back up all current files on your hard drive.

➢ Update all your Apple hard disks with the new driver from the Disk Tools disk in order for virtual memory to work correctly. You do this by using the HDSC setup program.

➢ Run the compatibility checker to examine your set of applications and report any possible incompatibilities.

Installation from floppy disks and compact discs (CD) are the same except for having to swap the floppy disks as requested. To begin the installation, open the installer application on the install 1 disk. Then a standard installer screen will come up, providing you with options that can be installed.

The software will identify the model of Macintosh computer that is being used and will select the necessary files for that model. Make sure at this point that the disk named on the installer screen is the one from which you want the software installed. Installer will prompt you to change disks during the installation. When the screen indicates that the installation is successful, click on quit.

When navigating, recognize that System 7 looks at the world as though it were a hierarchical set of disks, folders, and files—all available under a top-level virtual folder called the desktop. The hierarchical nature of the desktop is reflected in the way files are arranged in a list to view.

One of the first things you will notice in the list are the triangles standing upright at the left side of your window. Clicking a triangle will cause the triangle to turn downward at the same time that the file next to it displays a list of its contents. If you double-click on a folder or a file, that item becomes the active window.

Some of the abilities you want to develop in working with System 7 include the ability to:

➢ View file organization on the desktop customize views

➢ Use the keyboard to navigate the desktop

➤ Use labeling to group files

➤ Use the find command to locate files

➤ Start multiple applications and switch between them

➤ Get help from the desktop

➤ Remove files using the trash icon

System 7 has a feature called virtual memory that allows users to extend their available memory by using a portion of the hard drive as a "virtual" extension to the system RAM. This allows the running of larger applications with less RAM than would otherwise be required.

Not all Apple systems are able to use this feature. Those that cannot include Macintosh Classic, Macintosh Portable, and Macintosh II. Although these Macs will run System 7, they cannot use virtual memory.

✳ Clean installs

A clean install is not an upgrade install, but a complete install of an operating system "from the ground up."

Here are the steps that must be performed when doing a clean install of the Macintosh Operating System:

➤ Verify availability of space on the hard drive.

➤ Make backups of all programs and files.

➤ Disable the old system folder by dragging the finder out of it. Make sure you put the finder somewhere it can be retrieved (like the desktop) if the installation fails.

➤ Restart the Mac and immediately insert the first installation disk, then run Installer.

➤ When Installer has finished, restart the system again, and the new system will load.

➤ Drag all non-Apple extensions, control panels, preferences files, and fonts (if your old system was version 7.1 or later) from the old system folder into the new system folder's icon, not its window.

➤ Drag any extra fonts, sounds, or keyboard layouts from your old system folder to the new one.

If System 7.1 or later was installed, run the System Update 3 to obtain the best performance possible.

⇨ Connecting the Mac to a network

Networks for Macs include inexpensive connections such as LocalTalk and/or AppleTalk, as well as more capable networks using the Ethernet protocol. (See Fig. 6-5.)

Figure 6-5

The Power Macintosh in architecture. Apple Computer, Inc., 1995. All rights reserved. Used with permission.

What follows are some of the many aspects that must be considered when networking in a Macintosh environment.

Network environments include:

- ➤ AppleTalk
- ➤ TCP/IP
- ➤ IPX (NetWare)
- ➤ DECnet

AppleTalk is the plug and play environment that is built into most Macintosh environments. A number of the technical issues, such as assigning workstation and network addresses, and routing messages between networks are handled automatically by software installations.

TCP/IP stands for transmission control protocol/Internet protocol and is typically used when the Macintosh is being run in a multi-vendor environment. In a Mac environment that uses TCP/IP, you need to specify a number of network settings, such as device addresses. (In contrast, AppleTalk takes care of those network settings automatically.)

IPX (NetWare) is the Novell operating system environment, which was created "from the ground up," rather than being based on System 6 or 7. This environment does not depend on any other operating system environment to work in conjunction with it. IPX is the protocol used in IPX (NetWare). IPX stands for Internetwork packet exchange.

DECnet was developed for Digital Equipment Corporation's (DEC) VAX minicomputers, which are used extensively in business and research. While many VAX systems have UNIX operating environments that use a TCP/IP protocol, others are running proprietary VAX operating systems using DECnet protocol. DECnet was developed through a technical alliance of Apple and DEC.

After protocols we must consider network topologies. These are:

> Daisy chain

> Bus

> Ring

> Star

Daisy chain is the topology used for AppleTalk/LocalTalk networks. This topology is created by simply stringing a series of cable connections from one computer to the next. Each end of this network topology is terminated by a resistive terminating plug.

In a bus topology network, devices are strung linearly along a single cable. Each computer system requires a tap which actually penetrates the cable insulation to make contact.

In the ring topology, the network cable makes a complete loop back to where it started, forming a circle, or ring.

A star topology has several cables converging at a central point, usually with only one device connected at the end of each cable run.

The cabling used in a network environment must also be a factor when setting up a new or connecting to an existing network. The cable chosen will affect transmission speed, maximum distance the cable can be run, and the maximum number of nodes per run of cable. Since the cabling can also lay the foundation for future network growth, the wrong decision can be costly when it comes time to expand your network.

Some of the cable setups are:

> ➤ Apple LocalTalk
> ➤ 10Base T Ethernet
> ➤ 10Base 2 Ethernet
> ➤ 10Base 5 Ethernet
> ➤ FDDI optical fiber

The cabling used for Apple LocalTalk will support a maximum of 30 nodes per segment a distance of 1,000 feet, and has a maximum transmission speed of 230.4 K/second.

10Base T Ethernet, twisted pair, will support a maximum of one node per segment a distance of 100 meters, and has a maximum transmission speed of 10 megabits per second.

10Base 2 Ethernet, thin-wire will support a maximum of 30 nodes per segment a distance of 189 meters, and has a maximum transmission speed of 10 megabits per second.

10Base 5 Ethernet, thick-wire, will support a maximum of 100 nodes per segment, a distance of 500 meters, and has a maximum transmission speed of 10 megabits per second.

FDDI, optical fiber will support a maximum of 500 nodes per segment a distance of 100 kilometers, and has a maximum transmission speed of 100 megabits per second.

Installing and upgrading

Sequence of system start-up

The system start-up of a Macintosh, like that of a PC, begins by accessing the ROM and initializing and testing the various hardware components of the system. If no hardware problems are detected, the Mac will display a happy Mac icon and strike a chord. All icons and sounds are stored in ROM.

One of the first things that the operating system does is to set up a system partition in RAM. After that, the CPU looks for a start-up disk that contains the system files. Next the operating system looks for the resource files in the system folder's extension folder, and then the files in the control panel folder. The finder application is loaded into RAM and starts. The finder locates any and all applications, after which the Macintosh is ready for use.

Keep in mind that much of this discussion is geared toward System 7 software. System extensions were called inits in versions before System 7, and control panels were known as cdevs (control devices).

Major components and their functions

The Macintosh operating system has many components:

> System folder. This contains the most important group of files on your Mac, including the systems and the finder, which the Mac needs in order to start up and run normally.

> Apple menu items folder. This folder stores everything that appears on the Mac's Apple icon menu.

➢ Clipboard file. This is where the Mac stores anything that has been cut or copied.

➢ Control panels folder. This folder stores utility programs that inform you how the Mac works. It is used for sound control and desktop patterns, and it establishes file sharing with other Macs.

➢ Control strips modules folder. This folder stores files that perform functions on the powerbook's control strip, providing the system has one.

➢ Disabled folders. These folders are created by extension manager utilities to hold files you may want to temporarily exclude from the system.

➢ Extensions folder. This folder stores all extensions that extend the capabilities of the regular system software.

➢ Fonts folder. Stores all fonts loaded into the system.

➢ Finder. This creates the Mac desktop, with its menus.

➢ Launcher folder. All programs that you want to show up in the launcher window are put here.

➢ Preferences folder. This folder stores all preferences files that keep track of the options you have specified in the finder and in applications.

➢ Print/monitor documents folder. This is a holding area for temporary files the Mac creates when you print a document using background printing.

➢ Shutdown items folder. This is where you put files, program, or scripts that you want to run after you have selected shutdown. For example, you could design a script that automatically backs up files you were working on and puts them in this folder.

⇨ Common inits and extensions

In the Macintosh OS environment there are two main types of extensions. An extension is software that extends the system's capabilities. The two types are system extensions and chooser extensions.

System extensions, also referred to as inits in the System 6 environment, are loaded into memory at the time of system start-up. You can visually make sure these extensions are being loaded since they will be displayed along the bottom of the screen. In order to work properly, extensions must be loaded with the system; if a new one is added, you must reboot (restart) the system.

Chooser extensions, known as chooser devices (cdevs), show up as icons you can select in the chooser in order to set up connections through the Mac's modem and printer ports with networks of peripherals.

Never add extensions unless it is going to provide the end user with some real value. It is common in the microcomputer industry to add whatever is new or the latest fad, without considering compatibility with current operating environments.

Special boot procedures

At the time of power-up, a Macintosh system will scan the various drives within the system to find one that has a system folder. When it finds that drive, it will start to boot the system from it. There is a specific order in which the system searches the drives:

➣ The internal floppy

➣ Secondary floppy, if present

➣ External floppy, if present

➣ The disk specified in the start-up disk control panel

➣ The external serial, non-SCSI, hard drive

➣ The internal hard drive

➣ Other SCSI devices, including CD-ROMs and cartridges

If no system folder is found, the Macintosh system will wait approximately 15 seconds and start its search all over.

If it becomes necessary to preempt the normal booting of the internal drive, you could press the following key sequence: shift, option, Apple key, and delete.

Differences in Macintosh operating systems

As with other operating systems, the Macintosh OS systems have evolved through numerous versions. We discuss below System 6 and System 7. It is rare to find a Mac system with any release prior to System 6.

To find out the exact version of operating system you are dealing with, go to Finder and select "About this Macintosh," for System 7 or "About the Finder" in System 6.

One major difference between System 6 and System 7 is the ability to run more than one program at a time in System 7. Although System 6 environments can do this with Multifinder, the memory requirements are greater than they are with System 7.

Upgrading may not always be a good investment. For example, newer version operating environments typically require more hard drive space and might not work properly with older application software. However, if greater flexibility or the ability to run newer applications is important, then upgrading may be the best solution.

System 7 offered some of these new capabilities over System 6:

➤ Improved File Finder

➤ More versatile menus

➤ Easier font and sound installation

➤ Increase memory capacity from 8MB to 1 gigabyte under System 7

➤ Virtual memory

➤ New desktop features

Common application commands

You will find with Macintosh systems that many of the commands are common from application to application. Dialog boxes, alerts, text boxes, and buttons are very similar. If you do run into a confusing situation, you can always refer to the help menus, which are available only in System 7.

 # Major desktop features

The desktop type of interface is referred to as a graphical user interface (GUI), also pronounced "gooey." The desktop, of course, is analogous to a physical desktop on which one would lay out all the papers, files, and other objects one was working with.

The Macintosh desktop is what you see on the screen when you are in the finder. This includes the menu bar, background pattern, the trash icon, files, folders, and so on. Everything on the Macintosh desktop is manipulated by using the system's mouse to point and click on icons, which are graphic symbols representing different system features or applications.

It is from this desktop that you can organize the contents of your hard drive, launch program, or open documents. Finder also lets you modify your system setup by adding fonts, sounds, or changing settings in the control panels.

Macs have always been fun and there are a number of "desktop toys" that can be added to your system. Some of the more popular shareware toys are:

➤ *Aurora,* which adds color to your desktop

➤ *Eyeballs,* which puts a set of eyes in the menu bar which follow the cursor

➤ *MultiDog,* which has a ghost dog that runs around your icons.

 # Diagnosing

 ## Indicators of system malfunctions

Apple Macintosh, when working properly, will typically make a "boing" sound or a chord, followed by a smiling Mac icon as the system begins its initialization and boot-up process. Seeing a sad Mac in place of the smiling one could be an indication of a hardware failure. Along with the sad Mac, the Macintosh will play an ominous-sounding chord.

 ## Common error codes and start-up messages

Sad Mac: Usually an indication of some hardware failure.

Blinking question mark: Indicates that the Mac has passed its initial self-tests but cannot locate a disk with "boot blocks" and a working system. Make sure that all devices on your SCSI chain are powered on.

This is not a Macintosh Disk: This will appear when the OS does not recognize the format of the disk it is attempting to read.

If the happy Mac and "Welcome to Macintosh" message appears, but the system crashes before the desktop appears, try rebooting the system with the shift key held down. This will disable all extensions, including the control panels that have init resources in them.

 ## Isolating problems

If possible, it is always good to have a brief discussion with the operator of the machine. Whether the machine is a PC or a MAC, many—if not all—of the questions for the operator will be the same.

The main intent of your questions is to determine which of four areas the problem is occurring in. As mentioned in Chapter 4, those areas are:

➤ Hardware

➤ Software

➤ Environment (temperature, power, etc.)

➤ Operator error

Some questions you should be sure to ask:

➤ *Did you notice the error immediately at power-up or after the system had booted?* Some thermal problems exhibit themselves when the circuits are cold, others when the circuitry has been powered on a while. This question could also let you know whether the system failed power-on self-tests (POSTs) or if some other possible software-related problem emerged after the system has booted.

➤ *Could you continue on after the error or did the system lock up?* This question helps determine if the error is recoverable or nonrecoverable. This does not mean that the error is more or less serious; it could, however, lead to the next question.

➤ *Did the system display an error message?* An error message can be looked upon as the computer "telling on itself." Usually it indicates whether the error occurred in memory, processing, or during an input/output (I/O) operation. Also, error messages may tell whether the error occurred in the operating environment or the application environment.

The more we become familiar with microcomputer environments, the easier it becomes to recognize where an error message originates. An easy way to familiarize yourself is to examine any operating system user guide. It will typically list the most common error messages.

➤ *Can you duplicate the error?* Error duplication is a key area to explore; if the error can be duplicated, it might indicate operator error.

➤ *Is the error intermittent or does it happen repetitively?* Repetitive errors are easier to track than intermittent ones. See if the error occurs during most operations or just certain ones. Even if an error is random during different operations, it may point to some common denominators.

> ➤ *What operation were you involved in when the error occurred, or what task were you doing?* If the operator was entering data, it could be a keyboard processing error. If the operator was attempting to print, there may be a problem with the printer or I/O port. An error while saving to file could point to a faulty drive. Questions like these can tell you where the problem may be, and if it might be environmentally caused, software-based, or result from an operator input error.

Note that many software-related errors are caused by configuration errors. People inadvertently modify or change a setting without realizing it. When investigating any problem, leave no stone unturned. You will, however, face some situations that escape explanation.

Correcting a software problem will generally require you to have access to the master diskettes or a current backup for the system. This is necessary to obtain specific device drivers. Always refer to the software documentation, if available.

Isolating and testing hardware devices

After talking to the operator to gather clues about the problem, shut down the system and verify that all your external cable connections are in place. Try to power the system up and observe if the sad Mac has disappeared from the screen. Next, insert a system floppy disk and see if that boots the system. If none of these steps remove the sad Mac, disconnect all external SCSI devices, making sure that all power is off when doing so. If sad Mac still shows his face after all this, it is time to open up the box.

Be sure to follow proper cautions for electrostatic discharge (EDS). No integrated circuit(s) (IC) or field replaceable units (FRU) should be handled out of their protective wrapping without following these procedures.

Many companies today have made anti-static procedures a requirement of employment, and some educate their customers on ESD procedures. This is so that they are aware of what service

personnel should be doing and can report it to the technician's company if proper steps are not taken.

The basic ESD procedures include the following:

❶ Be sure you have your anti-static kit. This kit contains:
- Wrist strap and attachment cord
- Anti-static mat
- Anti-static bags to transport electronic circuit boards and/or components

The whole purpose of this kit is to allow you to neutralize any difference of potential between you and the equipment you are working on.

❷ Lay out the anti-static mat, and place the computer on it. Put on you wrist strap, connect it to the computer, and connect the computer to the mat.

By doing this, any charge that has built up between you and the computer will be dissipated through the connection, and you will be at equal potential with the machine.

Besides the static prevention, if you are working on a customer's desk, the anti-static mat will protect the desk from any scratches caused by moving the machine around.

After you have followed the above steps, open up the machine. Go through the system and ensure that all modules, cables, and SIMMS memory modules are properly seated in their connectors. Check again to see if the sad Mac has disappeared.

If the sad Mac is gone, and you are now getting the proper power indicator, then power down the system and go on to inspect the inside of the machine for any dust or dirt and perform some preventive maintenance by vacuuming and/or cleaning the system. It might be a good idea, since the system is open, to re-seat all connectors and/or modules in their connectors. If all of the above steps, including cleaning the machine, do not remove the sad Mac, more advanced diagnostic aids are necessary.

To aid in diagnosing faulty machines, Apple provides the Apple TechStep. This is a portable, hand-held testing device that diagnoses CPU systems and peripherals through their external ports. Apple TechStep is driven by a Motorola MC68HC11 8-bit single chip micro-controller. AppleTech Step does not require the power, video, or floppy drive, mouse, or keyboard to be functioning for it to aid in troubleshooting.

The most valuable tool in diagnosing any problems is a good set of disk-based diagnostics. Many vendors, including Apple, have software utilities available to assist you in testing and verifying the performance of Macintosh systems. Diagnostics are a time-saver for intermittent problems since they can be set up to continuously loop. Let the tests run overnight, logging recoverable errors as they go.

When troubleshooting an Apple system, you will need knowledge in these areas:

➢ Desktop and setup

➢ System software

➢ Understanding SCSI (Small Computer Systems Interface)

➢ Peripheral interconnection

 # Repairing

 ## Identifying needs for a repair

When repairing any system, if there are a number of options installed, it is a good practice to put the system back to its minimum factory configuration in order to isolate the base system from any options that have been added. These options could include modems, additional memory devices, or network cards.

When dealing with any bus system, these options, if they have a problem, could prevent the rest of the system from performing as it should. If the system begins to function without problems after

removing the options, it is a good sign that the problem is in one of those options. If the system still fails after removing the options, the base system is at fault.

It is always helpful to have some type of diagnostic software available when troubleshooting computer systems. (Of course, diagnostics are only useful if the system will initialize and boot.) Software such as Peace of Mind by Diagsoft, or Disk First Aid by Apple are good examples of software diagnostics available in the marketplace.

 # Sample test questions

What follows are sample test questions (and answers) for the Macintosh OS-based computers specialty exam. Each sample test question in this chapter comes from one of the same three sources as the test questions at the end of Chapter 4 (Self Test Software, CompTIA, or the authors), and all credits are similarly given. See page 152 in Chapter 4 for more information about these sources.

1. If a Macintosh computer has one internal hard drive, what is the maximum number of external SCSI devices that can be connected to the computer? *(Authors)*
    a. 3 devices.
    b. 5 devices.
    c. 6 devices.
    d. 8 devices.

2. In a Macintosh system, how does a hard drive start-up disk differ from a hard drive that is not a start-up disk? *(CompTIA)*
    a. A start-up hard drive must be initialized with a special file system.
    b. The start-up drive contains the system file and Finder applications.
    c. The start-up hard drive must have an interleave ratio that matches the computer, but a disk that is not a start-up disk can have a different interleave ratio.
    d. The start-up hard drive must be connected directly to the computer; hard drives that are not start-up disks can be daisy-chained.

3. In a Macintosh system, when the computer cannot access the hard disk, it will not show the disk's icon on the desktop. This could be the result of what? *(Authors)*
   a. A corrupt application.
   b. Not enough RAM.
   c. Fragmented desktop.
   d. A corrupt driver.

4. A customer complains that a lot of paper jams are occurring on her LaserWriter printer. What are possible causes that can be fixed by the customer? Choose all that apply. *(CompTIA)*
   a. Fuser assembly too hot.
   b. Too much paper in cassette.
   c. Paper size incorrectly indicated in 'Page Setup' dialog box.
   d. Paper that is damp or wrinkled.
   e. Dirty fuser cleaning rod.

5. In a Macintosh environment, when problems occur in many applications, it is possible that what is happening? *(Authors)*
   a. RAM memory is not sufficient.
   b. System file is corrupted.
   c. System folder is missing.
   d. Hard disk driver is corrupted.

6. If, after you connect a color monitor to a Macintosh, the picture is still in black and white, you should do what to correct it? *(Authors)*
   a. Set configuration switches inside the Macintosh.
   b. Re-boot the system.
   c. Choose Monitors Control Panel and select colors.
   d. Check cable connections.

7. What is not a necessary step when installing the System 7 software? *(Authors)*
   a. Back up the hard drive.
   b. Run MultiFinder.
   c. Run compatibility checker.
   d. None of the above.

8. Clicking on a triangle in the desktop screen in System 7 will cause what? *(Authors)*
   a. The triangle to point downward and close that window.
   b. No change in the triangle and reduce the window size.

    c. The triangle to point downward and expand the list.

    d. All of the above.

9. A Macintosh PowerBook's main battery will not recharge while the computer is connected to a known-good power adapter and power source. Replacing the battery does not solve the problem. Of the components listed below, which is most likely to be at fault? *(CompTIA)*

    a. RAM expansion card.

    b. Logic board.

    c. Keyboard.

    d. Modem on/off PC b.

10. Which of the following statements is true? *(Authors)*

    a. Two SCSI devices connected to a Macintosh computer can have the same SCSI ID as long as both devices are hard drives.

    b. Each SCSI device must have its own ID.

    c. All SCSI devices must have the same ID.

    d. SCSI ID numbers are irrelevant if the devices are connected to a Macintosh computer.

11. To delete files from the disk, you must do what? *(Authors)*

    a. Click on the trash icon.

    b. Drag the folder over to the trash icon.

    c. Do not save them.

    d. Keep files open at time of power-down.

12. Which operating system element provides the Macintosh user interface for all applications? *(Self Test Software)*

    a. A CDEV.

    b. The toolbox.

    c. The installer.

    d. A desk accessory.

⇨ Answers to sample questions

1. C	4. B,D	7. B	10. B
2. B	5. A	8. C	11. B
3. A	6. C	9. B	12. B

Cornerstone funding and sponsoring partners

The following lists of funding and sponsoring partners are valid as of October 1995.

Funding partners

American Institute

Apple Computer, Inc.

AST Research

AT&T Global Information Systems (formerly NCR/AT&T)

Compaq Computer Corporation

Computer Reseller News (CMP Publications, Inc.)

CompuCom Systems Inc.

CompUSA

Conner Peripherals

Data Train Institute

Digital Equipment Corporation

Entex Information Services

Exide Electronics Group Inc.

GE Information

Hayes Microcomputer Products, Inc.

Hewlett-Packard Company

IBM Education & Training

IBM PC Company, N.A.

InaCom Corporation

Ingram Micro Inc.

Intel Corporation, Inc.

Intelligent Electronics, Franchise Division, Inc.

Learning Tree

Lotus Development

MicroAge Inc.

Microsoft Corp.

Packard Bell Electronics

PC Week (Ziff-Davis Publishing)
Service News
Systems & Support Management
Tandy Services/Computer City
Technology Service Solutions
Toshiba America Information Systems, Inc.
U.S. Robotics, Inc.
VAR Business (CMP Publications, Inc.)
Wave Technologies
Zenith Data Systems/Groupe Bull

Sponsors

Aerotek-Data Services Group
American Power
Aurora/Century Computer Marketing
Banctec Service Corp.
Computer Curriculum Corporation
Epson America, Inc.
GE Capital Technology Service
Heath Co.
Lexmark
OKIDATA
PC Parts Express
Permond Solutions Group Inc.
Self Test Software
SHL Technical Service
TechForce
Total Seminars
VanStar
Wang Laboratories
Wurts & Associates

B

Becoming an
A+ Authorized
Service Center

To recognize the commitment that a variety of organizations have made to customer service and to the A+ program, CompTIA issues the designation of A+ Authorized Service Center to those locations that have 50% or more of their computer service technicians A+ certified. As of October, 1995, 1,182 service centers had earned the designation.

To become an A+ Authorized Service Center, your company must fill out the form that comes with the kit each candidate receives from Drake Prometric when he or she becomes A+ certified (the same kit in which you receive your lapel pin and certificate). Then return the form by mail or fax to:

Computing Technology Industry Association (CompTIA)
450 East 22nd St., Suite 230
Lombard, IL 60148
(708) 268-1384 (f)

The application must be filled out completely, and you need to give the verification number for each A+ certified technician, and indicate the total number of computer service technicians on staff. With properly completed paperwork, your organization should receive its A+ Authorized Service Center certificate and decal within three weeks.

Figure B-1

The A+ Authorized Service Center certificate.
CompTIA

Recommended
books and films

One of the following lists includes books and films to help you prepare for the A+ exams. This list incorporates the recommendations of dozens of IT trainers, managers, technicians, and consultants, all of whom are intimately familiar with the content of the A+ exams.

The second list includes book titles to help you in your career. These books cover the topics of job networking, resumes and cover letters, interviewing, and job opportunities for computer professionals.

Books and films for exam preparation

Computers (general)

Gertler, Nat. *Computers Illustrated.* Carmel, IN: Que Corp., 1994.

White, Ron. *How Computers Work.* Emeryville, CA: Ziff-Davis Publishing, 1992.

Hardware

Minasi, Mark. *The Complete PC Upgrade and Maintenance Guide, 4th edition* (book and CD). Alameda, CA: Sybex, 1995.

Mueller, Scott. *Upgrading & Repairing PCs, 4th edition.* Carmel, IN: Que Corp., 1994.

Norton, Peter. *Outside The IBM PC and PS/2: Access to New Technology.* Englewood Cliffs, NJ: Brady, 1992.

Rosch, Winn L. *The Winn L. Rosch Hardware Bible.* Englewood Cliffs, NJ: Brady, 1994.

DOS

Gookin, Dan. *DOS for Dummies, 2nd edition.* San Mateo, CA: IDG Books Worldwide, 1993.

Harvey, Greg. *DOS for Dummies Command Reference.* San Mateo, CA: IDG Books Worldwide, 1993.

Harvey, Greg. *DOS for Dummies Quick Reference.* San Mateo, CA: IDG Books Worldwide, 1993.

Stiles, Diana, and Winston Nathaniel Martin. *Microsoft MS-DOS Step by Step* (covers versions 6.0 and 6.2). Redmond, WA: Microsoft Press, 1993.

Weixel, Suzanne. *MS-DOS 6 Quickstart/The Step-By-Step Approach.* Carmel, IN: Que Corp., 1993.

Wyatt, Allen L., W. Edward Tiley, and Jon Paisley. *Using MS-DOS 6.2.* Carmel, IN: Que Corp., 1993.

 Networking

Cohen, Alan M. *A Guide to Networking, 2nd edition.* Danvers, MA: Boyd and Fraser, 1995.

Derfler, Frank J., and Les Freed. *How Networks Work.* Emeryville, CA: Ziff-Davis Press, 1993.

Novell, Inc. *Netware System Interface Technical Overview.* Reading, MA: Addison Wesley Computer, 1990.

Novell, Inc. *Novell's Quick Access Guide to Netware 3.11 Networks.* Alameda, CA: Sybex, 1992.

Novell, Inc. *Novell's Quick Access Guide to Netware 3.12 Networks.* Alameda, CA: Sybex, 1993.

Novell, Inc. *Novell's Quick Access Guide to Netware 4.0 Networks.* Alameda, CA: Sybex, 1993.

Microsoft Windows

Christian, Kaare, and Pamela Drury Wattenmaker. *How Windows Work.* Emeryville, CA: Ziff-Davis Press, 1994.

Microsoft Corporation. *Microsoft Windows NT Resource Kit* (book and disks). Redmond, WA: Microsoft Press, 1993.

Microsoft Corporation. *Microsoft Windows 3.1 Resource Kit* (book and disks). Redmond, WA: Microsoft Press, 1994.

Rathbone, Andy. *Windows for Dummies.* San Matteo, CA: IDG Books Worldwide, 1993.

Macintosh computers

Datatech Institute, 429 Getty Avenue, Clifton, New Jersey 07015 (Phone: 201-478-5400, extension 2301-for the video department) offers a variety of courses worldwide and also two videos on Macintosh computers:

Troubleshooting the Mac, and *Advanced Troubleshooting for the Mac.*

Goodman, Danny, and Richard Saul Wurman. *Danny Goodman's Macintosh Handbook.* New York: Bantam Electronic Publishers, 1992.

Naiman, Arthur, Nancy E. Dunn, and Susan McCallister. *The Macintosh Bible, 4th edition.* Berkeley, CA: A Goldstein and Blair Book from Peachpit Press, 1992.

Pogue, David. *Macs for Dummies.* San Matteo, CA: IDG Books Worldwide, 1994.

Rietmann, Kearney, and Frank Higgins. *Upgrading & Fixing Macs for Dummies.* San Matteo, CA: IDG Books Worldwide, 1994.

Rizzo, John, and K. Daniel Clark. *How Macs Work.* Emeryville, CA: Ziff-Davis Press, 1993.

Vandersluis, Kurt, and Amr Eissa. *Troubleshooting Macintosh Networks: A Comprehensive Guide to Troubleshooting and Debugging Macintosh Networks* (book and disk). San Matteo, CA: M&T Books, 1993.

Customer interaction skills

Davidow, William H., and Bro Uttal. *Total Customer Service: The Ultimate Weapon.* New York: Harpercollins, 1990.

Davis, Edwin G. *Customer Relations for Technicians.* Mission Hills, CA: Glencoe/Macmillan McGraw-Hill, 1991.

Sewell, Carl, and Paul B. Brown. *Customers for Life: How To Turn That One-Time Buyer Into A Lifetime Customer.* New York: Pocketbooks, 1992.

Certification

Drake Prometric. *The Complete Guide to Certification for Computing Professionals.* New York: McGraw-Hill, 1995.

Books for career development

Bloch, Deborah Perlmutter. *How to Have a Winning Job Interview.* Lincolnwood, IL: VGM Career Horizons, 1991.

Bone, Jan. *Opportunities in CAD/CAM Careers.* Lincolnwood, IL: VGM Career Horizons, 1993.

Ettinger, Blanche. *Opportunities in Customer Service Careers.* Lincolnwood, IL: VGM Career Horizons, 1992.

Fry, Ronald W. *Your First Resume, 4th edition.* Franklin Lakes, NJ: Career Press Inc., 1995.

Jackson, Tom. *The Perfect Resume.* New York: Doubleday, 1990.

Jackson, Tom. *Guerrilla Tactics in the New Job Market.* New York: Bantam Books, 1993.

Jackson, Tom. *Tom Jackson's Interview Express.* Westminster, MD: Times Books, 1993.

Jackson, Tom. *Tom Jackson's Power Letter Express.* Westminster, MD: Times Books, 1995.

Lott, Catherine S, and Oscar C. Lott. *How to Land a Better Job, 3rd edition.* Lincolnwood, IL: VGM Career Horizons, 1994.

Medley, H. Anthony. *Sweaty Palms: The Neglected Art of Being Interviewed.* Berkeley, CA: Ten Speed Press, 1992.

Moore, David J. *Job Search for the Technical Professional.* New York: Wiley and Sons, 1991.

Stoodley, Martha. *Information Interviewing: What it is and How to Use it in Your Career.* Garret Park, MD: Garret Park Press, 1990.

VGM. *Resumes for High Tech Careers.* Lincolnwood, IL: VGM Career Horizons, 1991.

Wendleton, Kate. *Through the Brick Wall.* New York: Five O'Clock Books, 1994.

Yate, Martin. *Cover Letters That Knock 'Em Dead.* Holbrook, MA: Bob Adams, Inc., 1995.

Yate, Martin. *Resumes That Knock 'Em Dead.* Holbrook, MA. Bob Adams, Inc., 1995.

Yate, Martin. *Knock 'Em Dead, 1996: The Ultimate Job Seeker's Handbook, 9th edition.* Holbrook, MA. Bob Adams, Inc., 1996.

Additional classroom
and self-study courses

Note: Because of the increasing popularity of the A+ certification program, the number of training courses and study materials is constantly growing. In order to get the most up-to-date listing of the organizations that provide training and study materials for the A+ exams, contact CompTIA:

(708) 268-1818

(708) 268-1384 (f)

75300,2507@compuserve.com (e-mail)

CompTIA provides the following list as a service to potential A+ certification exam candidates, but neither CompTIA nor this publisher certify or recommend the trainings or self-study guides listed in this appendix as preparation for taking the A+ certification exams, and we make no determination, warranty, or guarantee on the content or completeness of these products.

Aerotek-Dataservices
2299 Perimeter Park Drive, Suite 140
Atlanta, GA 30341
(800) 733-9783

Classroom-based courses

American Institute
708 Third Avenue
New York, NY 10017
(212) 661-3500

Classroom-based courses; self-study materials

DataTrain Institute
301 Madison Avenue, 5th floor
New York, NY 10017
(800) U-DATATRAIN
(800) 832-8287
(212) 286-9596 (f)

Customized training programs

Faculty Limited
Unit 1, Silverglade Business Park
Leatherhead Road, Chessington Surrey, UK KT9 2NQ
Phone: 011 44 01372 749690
011 44 01372 737478 (f)

Classroom-based courses

Heathkit Educational Systems
455 Riverview Drive
P.O. Box 1288
Benton Harbor, MI 49023
(800) 253-0570

Self-study kit

IBM Education Company
3100 Windy Hill Road
Marietta, GA 30067
(800) IBM-TEACH, Ext. 999

Self-study kit

Permond Solutions Group, The
90 Matheson Blvd.
West Mississauga, ON L5R 3R3, Canada
(905) 712-3434

Classroom-based courses

Self Test Software
4651 Woodstock
Suite 203, M/S 281
Roswell, GA 30075-1686
(800) 200-6446

Disk-based practice test

Total Seminars, LLC
2715 Bissonnet, Ste. 508
Houston, TX 77005
(800) 446-6004
(713) 520-0784
(713) 520-0786 (f)

Classroom-based courses

Wave Technologies
10845 Olive Blvd., Suite 250
St. Louis, MO 63141-7777
(800) 828-2050
(314) 995-5767

Classroom-based courses, self-study, and computer-based materials

 # Colleges

Training to prepare for the A+ certification exams is also available at the following colleges and/or universities:

Long Island University School
of Continuing Studies
Brooklyn Campus University Plaza
Brooklyn, NY 11201-5372
(718) 488-1010

Course: A+ Certification: A Test Prep Course for Computer Repair Technicians

Triton College
2000 Fifth Avenue
River Grove, IL 60171
(708) 456-0300, ext. 3360 or 3985

Program: Computer Maintenance Advanced Certificate

A+ certification name and logo usage guidelines

The following guidelines are provided by CompTIA to those who have earned the A+ certification:

 # Identifying yourself

How you use the A+ certification name and logo is important. It reflects on the program itself and your organization. We urge you to use it proudly to signify your commitment to service quality and excellence. In addition, we encourage you to involve your entire organization in helping us to raise the profile and enhance the image of the computer service professional.

You have been provided with the general program logo as well as a customized logo to publicize and communicate your status in and/or relationship to the A+ certification program. The parameters for use of the A+ certification name and logo are as follows:

Certified professionals are authorized to use the name and logo on personalized business cards and correspondence (e.g., letterhead, resume, etc.)

Figure E-1

The A+ logo. CompTIA

A+ Authorized Service Center usage is similar to that of a Cornerstone Funding Partner/Sponsor. The words "<Company name> is proud to employ A+ certified technicians" may be used in conjunction with the customized service center logo. (See Fig. E-2.)

The A+ Authorized Service Center graphic. CompTIA

Figure E-2

Cornerstone Funding Partners or Sponsors are authorized to use the name and logo on advertising and other printed materials (e.g., letterhead, invoices, customer correspondence, brochures, billboards, etc.) The words "XXX is proud to be a Cornerstone Funding Partner (or Sponsor) of the A+ certification program" may also be used in conjunction with the logo in printed advertising, as well as in television and radio ads. (See Fig. E-3.)

Figure E-3

Cornerstone Funding Partners

Cornerstone Funding Partners

Sponsor

Sponsor

Four ways to set up the logo as a Funding Partner or Sponsor. CompTIA

All other wording used to identify a company and its relationship to A+ certification must be pre-approved in writing by The Computing Technology Industry Association.

Using the A+ certification name and logo

➢ The A+ name may only be used to denote the A+ Certification Program.

➢ The A+ logo may not be incorporated as part of a reseller, manufacturer or participant's name.

➢ If the name or logo is used on store signs, stationery, invoices or business cards, it must clearly communicate the affiliation with the A+ Certification Program. It must not be used in a fashion that makes it appear that the individual or organization is The Computing Technology Industry Association, the A+ Certification Program, or that the name and logo belong to the individual/organization in question.

➢ Embossing of the name and logo is permitted for special events and/or invitations provided that it is printed in the specified colors.

A+ certification logo requirements

➢ The A+ certification logo must be accurately shown in proper proportion and orientation; distorting or rotating the logo is not permitted.

➢ The logo must not be incorporated into any other mark or symbol nor be used as a border on or around any item.

➢ A+ must not be used in copy independently of the words "certification program."

➢ The A+ certification logo may only be printed in the following ways:
  • Solid black
  • PMS 221 (a color similar to magenta printed solid only)
  • Reversed out of black, PMS 221, or other solid color (logo appears white).

➢ When the words "the Computing Technology Industry Association" are used in conjunction with the A+ logo, they must be placed as shown in Fig. E-4.

➢ The minimum clear space required on all sides of the symbol is 0.25 inch. This is to avoid distracting or confusing visual elements, such as copy, design elements or photos.

> The minimum scale for general usage of the A+ logo is ¾ × ¾ inch; except for business cards (or when the logo is stripped in on advertising promoting something other than the A+ Certification Program), for which the minimum scale is ⅜ × ⅜ inch.

> Any time the words, "the Computing Technology Industry Association" are used in conjunction with the A+ logo, general Association guidelines must be adhered to. For first usage: "The Computing Technology Industry Association"; thereafter, either "The Industry Association" or "The Association." Never use initials preceding the name of the Association.

Figure E-4

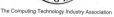

The Computing Technology Industry Association

The A+ logo done with the title in four different locations. CompTIA

Trademark/credit line requirements

The following trademark acknowledgment must appear on all printed advertising copy, and be included in any scripts, videos, or audio recordings:

"The Computing Technology Industry Association and A+ are registered trade marks. All rights reserved."

 # Other requirements

We recommend that there be at least one use of the following approved descriptive copy phrase for print advertising, brochures, or other collateral materials:

Computer Service Quality That You Can Trust

The following descriptive sentence must appear at least once on all advertisements, as well as be included in any scripts, videos or audio recordings:

A+ certification program is an industry-wide, vendor-neutral program developed and sponsored by the Computing Technology Industry Association.

 # Usage/activity pre-approval

Approval must be obtained prior to using the A+ certification name and logo in any way and for any activity, other than what is described in this brochure. Such approval is *always* given in writing.

To obtain copies of the A+ logo slicks (or get the logo on disk), please contact Elizabeth Berglund at CompTIA. Mock-ups, scripts, plan/promotion outlines or other appropriate samples for approval must be faxed (or mailed) to:

Ms. Elizabeth G. Berglund
Director of Marketing Communications
The Computing Technology Industry Association
450 E. 22nd St., Suite 230
Lombard, IL 60148
(708) 268-1384 (f)

In addition to the samples, the following information should accompany each submission:

> ➤ Contact name, name of organization, phone and fax number.

> ➤ Verification of relationship with the Computing Technology Industry Association.

> ➤ Scope of the planned use of the A+ name and logo.

For individuals or organizations that meet the criteria, approval is usually provided within 72 hours.

Computing Technology Industry Association
450 East 22nd Street, Suite 230
Lombard, IL 60148
(708) 268-1818
(708) 268-1384 (f)

F

The A+ job profile of a service technician

What follows is the job profile for computer technicians developed by CompTIA, in conjunction with its supporters from all areas of the IT industry. The profile identifies the major abilities required of service technicians at an entry level who have six months experience on the job.

Of the eleven categories of ability below, seven are tested on the current version of the A+ certification exam. Abilities related to customer interaction will soon be tested in a separate specialty exam designed exclusively for that purpose. And while abilities related to networking are not part of this list, future modules of the ever-evolving A+ exam will address networking skills.

Three categories listed on the job profile are not tested on the A+ exam because they do not lend themselves well to objective testing. These areas are business management skills, administrative skills, and professionalism. Following the job profile, each of these three is discussed for its importance in the work of a service technician.

Configuring

> ➤ Identify major components of the microcomputer and their functions.

> ➤ Identify major components of the display and their functions.

> ➤ Identify major components of the storage devices and their functions including SCSI devices.

> ➤ Identify major components of the printers and their functions.

> ➤ Identify major components of a local area network.

> ➤ Identify the components of various operating systems: DOS, System 7, OS/2, and Windows.

> ➤ Describe the system's RAM and ROM functions and capabilities.

> ➤ Follow the general steps for setting up (initializing) the system.

> ➤ Identify external connectors and ports.

> ➤ Test each part to be connected in the system, including the printer.

➤ Connect parts of the system, per specification.

➤ Verify that the system is properly set up.

➤ Boot the system, from diskette (all four operating systems).

➤ Identify functions of each operating system component (internal commands, external commands).

➤ Initialize, format, back up the diskette drive and hard disk drive, per operating system.

➤ Disassemble the system for shipment to customer.

➤ Practice sound safety procedures to reduce risk of ESD.

⇨ Installing and setting up

➤ Install all microcomputer components (CPU, motherboard, floppy drives, video controller, I/O ports, modem, power supply, mass storage devices, memory).

➤ Perform complete system checkout upon completion of installation.

➤ Connect peripherals (external drive, printer, etc.).

➤ Explain to the customer the basic functions of what is installed and what has been done to the system.

➤ Inspect all components of the system.

➤ Install, set up, and cable the system at the customer site, including setting switches and jumpers, with peripherals, operating system and communications interface, per spec.

➤ Connect the system to network and verify communications within the network.

➤ Use self-diagnosis and other testing techniques/tools to optimize (tune) the system performance.

➤ Perform machine moves at the customer site.

➤ Practice sound safety procedures and reduce risk of ESD.

⇨ Upgrading

➤ Install new basic version of software (operating system and device drivers, not applications) on existing systems.

➤ Install new microcomputer components, including ROM and SCSI devices, on existing systems.

➤ Install new display components on existing systems.

➤ Install new storage media components on existing systems.

➤ Install new printer components on existing systems.

➤ Practice sound safety procedures and reduce risk of ESD.

➤ Maintain a level of awareness of existing and potential customers and/or machine problem situations.

➤ Verify system operation.

⇨ Diagnosing

➤ Question customer to determine details of service situation.

➤ Use visual and audio indicators of system malfunction.

➤ Identify problems (failures) as customer sees it; that is, recreate the problem.

➤ Determine (hypothesize) the hardware, software, environment and/or operator as the cause(s) of the problem.

➤ Confirm the working elements of the hardware, software, and the system, including following the standard test procedures for microcomputers, displays, storage media, and printers to the FRU level.

➤ Identify probable actions to take to correct system failures (including problems with drivers, printer interfaces, printers, async communications, etc.).

➤ Determine when to use appropriate diagnostic tools, aids, test equipment.

➤ Use the tools, aids, and test equipment appropriately and effectively.

➤ Practice sound safety procedures and reduce risk of ESD.

 # Repairing

➤ Follow modular repair strategy.

➤ Follow steps in the repair process and standard procedures to remove and replace FRUs, repair machine failures, remove and replace modules (including cover, main board, power supply, SIMMS, video board, display, drives, chips, etc.), using appropriate safety and ESD procedures.

➤ Repair printer failures, using standard procedures.

➤ Verify problem is fixed.

➤ Explain the function performed by each replaceable service module.

➤ Reassemble, clean, and adjust system.

➤ Prepare system for shipping.

➤ Solder as needed to accomplish high reliability work.

➤ Identify proper tools, aids, test equipment, for safe and appropriate use.

 # Interacting with customers (not currently tested in A+)

➤ Display a high degree of tact, ethics, and courtesy to promote good customer relations that express professional business attitudes and experience, including:
  • own the problem
  • know when to escalate problems to higher authority
  • recognize sales situations

➤ Disengage at completion of customer interaction, including transferring requests to other professionals as needed, for example, respond to customer service requests on appropriate equipment.

➤ Notify customer for purpose of scheduling and explaining status of repair job.

➤ Seek information from customers related to problems leading to service request.

➤ Explain the service procedures, quality standards, customer service commitment, if requested by the customer.

➤ Address customer needs in a timely fashion, to minimize disruption to customer operations.

➤ Inform customer of the distinctions between billable activities, warranties, and contract.

➤ Work well under pressure.

Performing preventive maintenance

➤ Implement proactive preventive maintenance procedures as required, depending on vendor or environmental conditions, including inspections, testing, cleaning, adjusting, that minimize disruption to customer operations at a time of service call.

Maintaining safety

➤ Use preventive equipment to reduce the risk of damage from ESD, knowing when and when not to as well as why.

➤ Follow and implement standard safety procedures.

➤ Recognize how and why to use tools (basic devices and procedures) and test equipment.

 Other

Business management skills (not tested in A+)

> ➤ Keep management informed of existing or potential customer or machine problems.

> ➤ Determine whether a given situation is covered by warranty, contract, or time and materials.

> ➤ Report problems and customer dissatisfaction to management.

> ➤ Communicate to supervisor the most common failures.

> ➤ Plan and order the correct parts, as needed.

> ➤ Submit work orders promptly and accurately.

> ➤ Deliver, load, unload, count and organize the service center inventory.

 Administrative skills (not tested in A+)

> ➤ Complete service paperwork accurately and on time.

> ➤ Maintain organized records and failure analysis data.

> ➤ Prioritize and schedule the workload on a daily basis to ensure customer satisfaction, making optimum use of time and productivity.

Professionalism (not tested in A+)

> ➤ Keep abreast of all products through study of manuals and bulletins and through continuing education.

The last three areas mentioned above, though not tested on the A+ exams, are nevertheless important to the work of the service

technician. Understanding and being able to discuss the key tasks in each area will help you when preparing for a job interview and planning your career progress. Each is discussed briefly below:

Business management skills

Proper business management is central to the service technician's job. You must understand your role and your effect on the company's bottom line. For example, if you provide free warranty work for a customer and later find out the product wasn't covered by warranty, you have cost your employer money. The manufacturer will not reimburse your employer. If you encounter a part failure repeatedly, you should report it to your manager. Your manager will contact the vendor and get reimbursement for defective parts.

You will be tasked with keeping your manager aware of existing or potential customer or machine problems. Report these problems to management. Part of business management is determining whether a service call is covered on a warranty, contract, or time and materials basis, and then ensuring that the customer understands the billing charges.

Service technicians are closely involved in parts management. In your job, you may participate in planning what parts are needed, and ordering them. Your job may also include parts delivery, unloading, and counting parts, as well as organizing the service center inventory.

Administrative skills

Administration encompasses the paperwork, follow-up, and record-keeping essential to the job. Most of us do not like paperwork, but it is an important part of a service technician's job. Your employer will expect service paperwork completed accurately and on time.

Your ability to set priorities and manage your time and workload efficiently, making the best use of your time, will help to ensure that you produce the results your employer expects.

 # Professionalism

In the constantly changing IT field, your knowledge and skills need to be continually updated. Take the time to read about developments in the field and take additional training when needed.

Professionalism also involves skills in customer interaction. Maintaining a professional attitude during customer transactions and with co-workers is a must.

Consider how these areas of responsibility affect you in your present job and how they might be involved in your future work. Review the duty areas listed under these headings and prepare to be asked about them during job interviews. You might also take the initiative to ask an interviewer or potential employer (outside of an interview) what they expect of qualified service technicians on their staff in the areas of business management, administration, and professionalism.

Research on the value of certification

The following material is provided for those who would like a deeper understanding about the importance of certification to all of the players in the IT industry, and a look at some of the research that documents it. This material may develop your appreciation both for the A+ certification and for other certifications that you may choose to pursue in your professional development.

The IT professional

One reason for certification growth is the belief of IT professionals that holding the credential will advance their careers. How widespread is this belief?

A landmark study called "Technical Training and Certification: Outlook and Opportunities," conducted by the research firm Dataquest Worldwide Services of Framingham, Massachusetts, gives insights on the views about certification held by all the players in the IT industry. The study shows that certification candidates believe certification will bring them a variety of benefits including opportunities for new jobs and promotions. Respondents also believe that employers and customers will respond to them more favorably as a result of their certification.

Virtually all of the professionals in the Dataquest study considered certification to be of value to their careers; many considered it very valuable. (See Fig. G-1.)

The majority (55.8%) of certification candidates responding also believe that certification will be a significant help in getting a desired job in the future. Most of them also are pursuing certification as a ticket to advancement in their profession or in their current job. (See Fig. G-2.)

Many believe that certification will enhance their image within their organization and with customers. (See Fig. G-3.)

How closely do those beliefs of IT professionals match reality? Dataquest again provides some insights. The study suggests that the certified professional's salary and position will in fact, be advanced because of the certification. Managers in the study made comments such as these: "There is an automatic add-on to certified employees' salaries"; "There

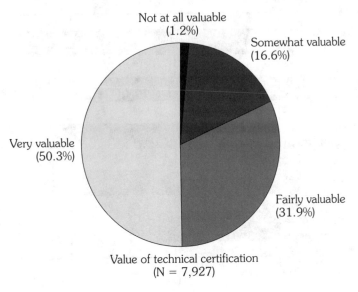

Not at all valuable
(1.2%)

Somewhat valuable
(16.6%)

Very valuable
(50.3%)

Fairly valuable
(31.9%)

Value of technical certification
(N = 7,927)

Candidates see high value in certification. Dataquest, 1995

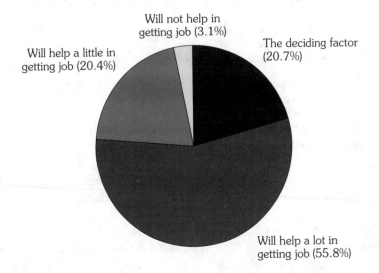

Will not help in
getting job (3.1%)

Will help a little in
getting job (20.4%)

The deciding factor
(20.7%)

Will help a lot in
getting job (55.8%)

Expected influence of certification
in getting desired job in future
(N = 5,877)

Most candidates believe that certification will help in getting future jobs. Dataquest, 1995

Figure G-3

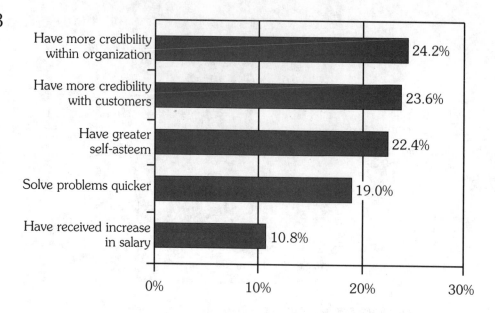

Achievements as a result of certification (N = 7,398)

Note: Multiple responses permitted.

Many believe that certification will enhance image within the organization and with customers. Dataquest, 1995

is a salary increase or bonus for achieving certification"; and, "We give certified employees more responsibility and higher pay."

Beyond the evidence provided by the Dataquest study, hiring trends also seem to reflect a preference for certified candidates.

Vicki Balser of Kelly Services, Technical Division, says that overall, companies are looking for IT professionals either right out of school with strong potential or specific technical skills; for example, with applications or client/server environments. Balser estimates that most of the technical skills sought today are network-related.

The Dataquest study suggests that the technical positions most likely to require certifications are System and Network Engineer. (See Fig. G-4.)

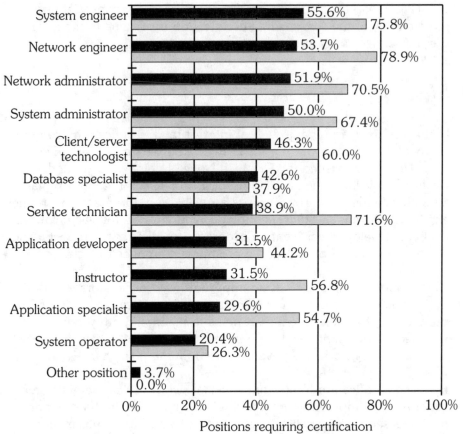

Note: Multiple responses permitted.

■ Corporate (N = 54)   □ Reseller (N = 95)

System/network engineer and administrator positions most likely to require certification. Dataquest, 1995

Balser believes that certifications can play an important role in an IT professional's job search, but for most job seekers, she says, it is not the certification alone, but certification plus experience that will do the trick. That belief was echoed by respondents in the Dataquest study, many of whom believe that certification does not substitute for experience.

The IT job market is receptive to those with certifications. Let us look more closely at the reasons that certification is of value to those who use the services of IT professionals.

 # Vendors

In the last six years, the growth of interest in IT certification programs has been led in large part by software and hardware vendors. Ever since Novell established the Certified Novell Engineer (CNE) and Certified Novell Instructor (CNI) programs in 1989, the industry has taken to the idea of certification as a reliable measurement for product expertise. Dozens of other technology vendors have followed Novell's lead and developed certification programs for their own products; and the number of vendor-sponsored programs continues to increase.

Certification has emerged as an important way for vendors to ensure that resellers and service providers have the knowledge to use the products to their full potential. It helps to promote both product knowledge and service and support skills—all of which have increased in importance as systems have increased in complexity.

By using certification to qualify individuals who service their customers, vendors have improved repeat and referral business, both accounting for increased revenues. For many vendors, certification has meant more satisfied customers and a more successful distribution chain.

Also, with budgets squeezed, vendors want their training to have the most impact with the least expenditure. Certification programs help boost training impact by developing a practical job focus for the training programs that prepare students for those exams.

For example, Nancy Lewis of Microsoft says that Microsoft's authorized support centers value certification for the way it sets goals for their training programs. She says that the centers are telling Microsoft, "Now we know what to train our people on and, with certification, we know when we are done." Lewis says, "That sounds like a simple thing, but it can help you to be much more efficient with your money."

Resellers

Resellers of IT products have taken enthusiastically to certification. Here are several reasons why:

❋ Customers prefer certified resellers

According to a study by International Data Corporation in October, 1993, customers prefer to receive service from value added resellers (VARs) that hold formal vendor certifications. The study showed that users believe certified VARs "tend to know their products better, have more training, and can provide better training when we need it."

Users also indicated to IDC that they appreciate their certified resellers because they believe these resellers have a closer relationship with manufacturers. They believe that certified resellers get better support from the manufacturer and thus have the ability to provide superior support to the customer.

❋ Certification provides managerial benefits to resellers

Managers at the reseller level often want to inventory the skills of their staff. They want their talent to be well distributed geographically and to offer, collectively, all of the skills each region requires. Certification results help managers to catalog skills, and thereby deploy them more effectively.

Certification also helps the manager to advance employees and to discriminate among them regarding their long-term worth.

❋ Certification is often a vendor requirement

Service-oriented resellers are increasingly required by vendors to have certified technicians on staff to service vendor products. Among the sample in the Dataquest certification study, 29% of resellers indicated that vendors required them to have certified technicians on staff.

From the vendor's perspective, professional certification can be a measure of the reseller's commitment to the vendor's products. It shows that the reseller is committed to delivering high-quality solutions using those products.

The popularity of certification for resellers is also clearly shown in IDC's reseller survey. Figure G-5 shows the percentage of employees certified by reseller size, 1993. All resellers in the survey said they would significantly increase the number of certified staff in 1994. Figure G-6 shows reseller perceptions about certification as a competitive advantage.

Figure G-5

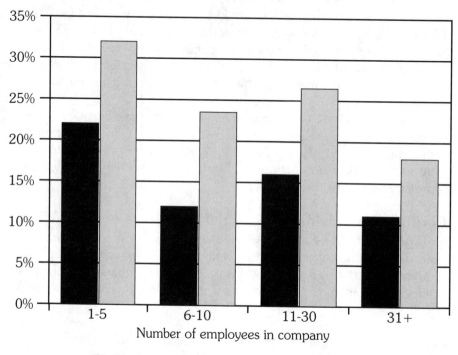

% of staff with advanced network certification

% of staff to be certified within 12 months

Percent of employees certified, by reseller size (1993). International Data Corporation

Nearly 60% of the resellers surveyed in the Dataquest study require certification for everyone on staff, and 25% require it for their most senior employees.

Resellers believe in and endorse certification, and often view it as a requirement for doing business. Their involvement with certification will clearly increase as time goes on.

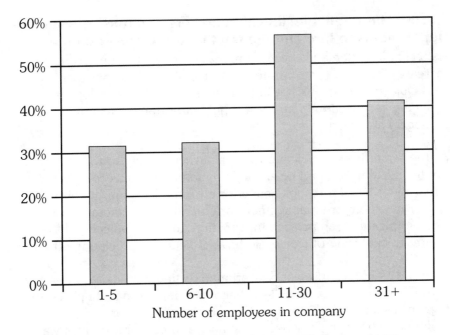

Percent of resellers believing that certification offers a competitive advantage, by reseller size (1993). International Data Corporation

 # End users

The organization that is the ultimate "end user" of IT skills can be a business, association, or government agency. And that organization usually includes a number of departments for technical work, training, and human resource management. Each of these departments, and the organization as a whole, benefits from the certification of IT professionals.

Certification helps end-user organizations in two fundamental ways: first, in selecting employees and contractors with the needed skills; second, in making the best use of human resources.

Here are some of the specific benefits that departments in the end-user organization enjoy.

✷ **Certification helps technical managers and human resources departments to hire and contract with the most qualified**

As technology demands become more complex and support demands increase, the need for accurate and quick hiring decisions increases too. Objective and consistent methods of evaluating employees, including certifications, are increasingly important to technical managers and recruiters.

At the same time, certification offers particular help to the nontechnical manager. For example, when a human resources department has the responsibility for a hiring decision, the hiring officer may be more management-oriented than technology-oriented. The certification can provide information about technical skill that a nontechnical hiring officer could have difficulty appreciating otherwise.

Stanford VonMayhauser of Educational Testing Service says that the certification of computer skills is becoming increasingly important to human resources departments. "Those responsible for human resources," he says, "are becoming aware of certification as a way to understand the quality of applicants. It gives information that is job-related, useful, valid, and reliable."

Human resources departments also benefit from objective evaluation methods. Certification is often seen as providing accurate and consistent measures of skill—something that training programs alone rarely provide. Certification testing ensures candidates an equal and fair chance to demonstrate their skills. This minimizes the risk of litigation over issues of hiring, promotions, and layoffs.

The Dataquest study indicated that the majority of resellers and corporate customers, including both technical managers and HR departments, believe they get more value out of certified employees. Those employees are seen as having greater self-esteem, providing higher levels of service and productivity, and playing a leadership role for other employees.

✷ **Certification helps ensure that the right person is in the right job**

Project planning becomes more realistic for both the short- and long-term when managers know the skill sets they have access to. And

certifications help managers to inventory those skills. Certification creates a framework for determining job skills, job levels, and career paths.

The information provided by certification helps managers to better fit employees to appropriate jobs and makes it easy to link reassignment or compensation to competency. Once hired, an employee can be tested and recertified or attain new certifications at more advanced levels or in related disciplines to qualify for promotions. Certification also facilitates retraining to work effectively in other areas of the company as organization requirements change.

Certification may help lower operating costs and increase productivity by ensuring that the right person is in the right job. Placing an employee in the proper niche produces long-term job satisfaction and a lower turnover rate among incumbents as well as new hires.

✳ Certification supports the end-user's training and development efforts

Certification programs offer end-user training departments the opportunity to verify through the quantifiable results of certification exams that learning has, in fact, resulted from training. Certification scores can help determine if training programs are meeting their development goals and if candidates are learning information vital to their positions. Demonstrating results to management through such objective means is increasingly important to HR and training & development departments.

But certification does more to help training departments than just document with numbers that key skills are being mastered. It helps the training department to become more efficient in several ways. For example, certification scores can help training departments determine if further training is needed.

Also, feedback from score reports can help students identify specific areas that remain to be mastered and focus their efforts on these. And when unnecessary training is eliminated, the end user saves significantly on travel, course costs, and downtime.

Training on demand is also more stimulating for learners. Employees prefer programs directed very specifically at their individual needs

rather than the needs of a department or other group to which they belong. Thus certification programs stimulate interest in training and help training departments build both interest in employee development, and also demand for training department programs.

External certification programs may help training department efficiency in another way: they may be testing and developing knowledge that is more useful for the end user than what its own internal training and testing programs deliver. One reason for this is that exams of external certification programs reflect a standard of performance on particular technologies held by the IT industry as a whole, rather than the narrower standards of a single company.

Also, certification exams are typically related to the particular knowledge, skill, and ability to perform a real-world job, rather than the knowledge to pass a single course of study only.

✳ Certification can help end-user organizations win strategic advantage

Certification can help companies in ways that go beyond helping individual departments. As such, certification becomes a strategic tool for building the company as a whole.

For example, companies employing certified IT professionals sometimes find that the company's recruiting efforts are enhanced as a result. Many job seekers are impressed by the fact that the company has a large cadre of certified staff. It makes them feel that they will have a group of expert colleagues with whom to share knowledge.

Certification can also help with company advertising, particularly when the company is offering services related to information technology. The commitment to certification can easily be read by the market as a commitment to technical excellence.

Certification can also foster team building and a sense of collegiality among IT staff. It may also promote better relations between internal technology support staff and the internal audience of company computer users they provide service to. Training for certifications keeps service providers on the cutting edge of knowledge, and their

credential can bring them respect and cooperation from internal users just as it can from the external marketplace.

The rapid growth of certification is explained by a simple fact: it works to protect and advance the interests of all the major players in the industry.

Certification helps vendors ensure quality service and support to their products. It helps industry resellers set themselves apart from the competition with superior product knowledge and service. Certification helps professionals to verify to potential employers the knowledge and skill they can bring to a job. It helps end-user organizations to select, train, and deploy workers more effectively. Certification also helps IT associations to protect the integrity of the industry and to advance the interests of individual professionals through standards of professionalism.

Index

Illustrations are in **boldface.**

About the authors

Sarah T. Parks has more than 20 years of support and training experience, including 10 years in customer support and training management at Apple Computer, Inc. Most recently, she was Director of Client Services at Dataquest. Ms. Parks is a former co-chair of the A+ Certification Program Advisory team. She has a B.S. in organizational behavior and currently works at C&S Services, a consulting services and software development organization, where she is responsible for training and customer support consulting.

Bob Kalman is Dealer Support Manager for North America for Zenith Data Systems. He has also served as a Senior Technical Training Specialist for Zenith, a Field Service Engineer for MCC Powers, and a Support Technician for GTE. Mr. Kalman was co-chair of the service section committee and a member of the A+ certification working team during the initial stages of A+ exam development. He became A+ certified in 1993 and holds numerous other certifications. Mr. Kalman has taught electronic technologies and computer repair at Oakton Community College in Des Plaines, Illinois, and at Triton College in River Grove, Illinois. He has more than 20 years experience with electronics, microcomputers, and information technology training. In addition, he is the author of *Microcomputer Repair* (1987), published by Heath/Zenith.